MACHINE
LEARNING
UPGRADE

MACHINE LEARNING UPGRADE

A Data Scientist's Guide to MLOps®, LLMs, and ML Infrastructure

KRISTEN KEHRER AND CALEB KAISER

WILEY

Library of Congress Cataloging in Publication data available on request.

Cover images: Neon: © bortonia9/Getty Images
         Background: © imaginima/Getty Images
Cover design: Wiley

SKY10078844_070324

Contents

Contents

Contents

Introduction

Welcome to a journey through the dynamic world of modern machine learning (ML)! In this book, we'll guide you from the data scientist's role with historical roots in business intelligence to the forefront of today's cutting-edge, multicomponent systems. You can find a GitHub with code examples from the book at `https://github.com/machine-learning-upgrade` so you can follow along.

We intend this book to be something you can read all the way through. This is not an index of methods or a comprehensive book on machine learning. Our aim is to cover the challenges associated with modern-day machine learning with a particular focus on data versioning, experiment tracking, post-production model monitoring, and deployment to equip you with the code and examples to start leveraging best practices immediately.

Chapter 1 lays the groundwork, revealing how the workflow for managing machine learning has evolved from traditional, more linear frameworks for data science like CRISP-DM to the advent of language model-powered applications, or large language models (LLMs). We set the stage by emphasizing the need for a unified framework that hints at the thrilling path ahead—building an LLM-powered application together.

As we delve into Chapter 2, prepare to witness an end-to-end approach to machine learning, exploring its life cycle, the principles of a production machine learning system and the core of our LLM application.

Chapter 3 zooms in on the data-centric view, emphasizing the role of data in modern ML. This is a hands-on chapter, where we create embeddings and harness the power of vector databases for text similarity searches. We couple ethical guidelines and data versioning strategies to ensure a responsible and comprehensive approach.

Then comes Chapter 4, where we guide you through selecting the right LLM, leveraging LangChain, and fine-tuning LLM performance.

With each part seamlessly connected, we venture into Chapter 5 to assemble our components and transition from prototype to application. We also demonstrate how to build dashboarding and application programming interfaces (APIs) to make your model results available to end users.

But it doesn't stop there. Chapter 6 completes the ML life cycle, tackling model monitoring, retraining pipelines, and envisioning future deployment strategies and stakeholder communication.

Finally, in Chapter 7, we recap the best practices uncovered throughout this journey, explore emerging trends in LLMs, and provide resources for further learning.

This book is more than a guide—it's an adventure, an invitation to traverse the landscapes of modern machine learning, and an opportunity to equip yourself with the tools and knowledge to navigate it. So, fasten your seatbelt, friends, and let's get going!

Acknowledgments

Writing this book has been a collaborative journey filled with shared vision and support from an incredible network of individuals who have made this possible.

We are immensely grateful to the team at Wiley, particularly James Minatel and Gus Miklos, whose dedication and expertise transformed our manuscript into a polished book. We appreciate your commitment to excellence.

Our profound appreciation goes to the technical editor, Harpreet Sahota, who provided invaluable feedback and challenged us to refine our ideas and improve the manuscript. Your insights and guidance were crucial in shaping the final book.

We extend our heartfelt thanks to the readers who will engage with our collective work. We hope this book offers valuable insights and sparks new ideas in your explorations.

To each person who has contributed, directly or indirectly, to this collaborative effort, thank you for being part of this journey.

With gratitude,

Kristen Kehrer

Caleb Kaiser

About the Authors

Kristen Kehrer has been a builder and tinkerer delivering machine learning models since 2010 for e-commerce, healthcare, and utility companies. Ranked as a global LinkedIn Top Voice in data science and analytics in 2018 with 95,000 followers in data science, Kristen is the creator of Data Moves Me. She was previously a faculty member and subject-matter expert at Emeritus Institute of Management. Kristen earned an MS in applied statistics from Worcester Polytechnic Institute and a BS in mathematics.

Caleb Kaiser is a full-stack engineer at Comet. Caleb was previously on the founding team at Cortex Labs. He also worked at Scribe Media on the author platform team and completed a BA of fine art in writing from the School of the Art Institute of Chicago.

About the Technical Editor

Harpreet Sahota is a self-described generative AI hacker. He earned undergraduate and graduate degrees in statistics and mathematics and has been in the "data world" since 2013, working as an actuary, biostatistician, data scientist, and machine learning engineer with expertise in statistics, machine learning, MLOps, LLMOps, and generative AI (with a focus on multimodal retrieval augmented generation). He loves tinkering with new technology and spending time with his wife, Romie, and kids, Jugaad and Jind. His book Practical Retrieval Augmented Generation will publish with Wiley in 2025.

## Chapter 1

A Gentle Introduction to Modern Machine Learning

Over the last 20 years, data science has largely been focused on using data to inform business decisions. Typical data science projects have centered around gathering, cleaning, and modeling data or creating a dashboard before finally producing a presentation to share results with stakeholders. This pipeline has been the backbone of many important business decisions. It has driven quite a bit of revenue. There have been many, many dashboards.

Traditionally, we might refer to the projects where we perform descriptive analysis to make informed decisions as *business intelligence* (BI). And in theory, BI is a specific field that is part of the data sciences. Data science *technically* refers more broadly to the practice of applying statistical methods (including modeling), coding, and domain knowledge to data, whereas business intelligence more narrowly applies to taking a data-driven approach to business decisions that focus more on descriptive and diagnostic analytics than the predictive analytics you might see from data scientists. However, we consider all analysts and BI professionals to be working in the "data sciences."

In practice, if you've had a job as an analyst or a data scientist in the last decade, you've probably spent a lot of time on business intelligence, in one way or another.

Many people might cry foul on this claim, pointing out that business intelligence, as we traditionally think of it, falls under the domain of roles with titles like "BI analyst," while data scientists tend to have more varied and research-focused responsibilities. While that might be true on some level, breaking down the responsibilities and functions of different roles in an average analytics organization makes it difficult to neatly separate data science from BI, and there will always be overlap when working with data.

For example, as an analyst at an average company, you'd likely be responsible for answering "what happened?" questions, using descriptive analytics to provide a snapshot of past performance. You might use Excel, SQL, and visualization software to generate reports and dashboards. You would likely monitor key performance indicators (KPIs) and help make strategic decisions based on historical data. There is also a chance that as a BI analyst or a business analyst the KPIs, data sources, and machine learning models (if any) used in this process are set up for you *before* you start the project—you manage them.

Now, when the company has completely new data to process, it is often made available via self-service for nontechnical stakeholders through yet another dashboard (this is where those excruciating debates about Tableau versus Power BI can crop up).

In general, this is a useful way to think about the distinction between data scientists and explicit BI roles at average companies. A data scientist will usually be responsible for the more technical, research-intensive projects in an analytics organization: exploring new data sources, implementing predictive analytics, performing hypothesis tests, researching new machine learning models, etc. However, much of what they do is still focused on, or in service to, what we can broadly define as business intelligence.

Or at least, this used to be the case.

Data Science Is Diverging from Business Intelligence

We should underline how research-focused data science work often is, especially when it comes to machine learning. In advanced analytics, where many data scientists' roles now sit; if you were to build a machine learning model, there is a good chance that the model would only ever be used for research. Years ago, in particular, it would be unlikely that you'd ever work on a model that was deployed or implemented in the product. You might build out a behavioral customer segmentation or build a predictive model with the goal being to understand your customers better. The new information about your customers might drive new features or changes to the product through further hypothesis testing. Still, the model itself might not be used any more once the research is communicated to the business.

This isn't because data scientists don't want to train models that have huge impacts; it's because this has historically just been *really hard*. In 2022, Gartner published a survey of companies using machine learning (ML) across the United States, Germany, and the United Kingdom, which found that only 54% of the models their data scientists developed ever made it to production, and that is after years of development within the ML ecosystem.

So instead, much of the actual business value delivered by data scientists has come from less "flashy" BI work, while their model building research has served primarily as résumé padding. But finally, this is starting to change.

Modeling itself has become more feasible, and it's becoming more common for it to be used in products. New tools like AutoML and improvements to existing ML frameworks have made it much easier for data scientists to train useful models on virtually any type of data. Transfer learning, popularized by computer vision and further spurred on by the explosion of large language models, has made training impactful models even easier in many respects. Even deployment has become more approachable as the ML infrastructure ecosystem has had time to develop.

As a result, data scientists are more and more working on modeling use cases that add to the business, and this is moving them away from traditional BI work. Increasingly, data scientists are responsible for building and monitoring machine learning models. This brave new world, however, has introduced an entirely new set of challenges and responsibilities for data scientists, and this is the core motivation of this book—to help you transition from the BI-focused world of data science to the new world, in which data scientists engineer production-focused, multicomponent machine learning systems.

Many of the principles covered in this book can be broadly referred to as MLOps (or LLMOps), but to be clear, our goal is not to become MLOps engineers, as it is not a data scientist's job to manage the tooling and infrastructure. The hope is instead that by understanding MLOps principles, data scientists can build reliable, scalable, and reproducible models that have real-world impact.

Before digging deeper into these principles, we should take some time to explore the changes in machine learning that have powered this transition.

From CRISP-DM to Modern, Multicomponent ML Systems

Machine learning has come a long way since its inception. In the 1990s, CRoss-Industry Standard Process for Data Mining (CRISP-DM) was introduced to describe the typical phases of a data modeling project. For a long time, it was the dominant framework for managing the machine learning workflow. CRISP-DM was instrumental in promoting the idea that data science should not be ad hoc but rather needed to be an organized process. The CRISP-DM framework featured six key steps:

1. **Business understanding:** Defining the objectives and requirements of the project from a business perspective.

2. **Data understanding:** Collecting and exploring the data to understand its quality and structure.

3. **Data preparation:** Cleaning, transforming, and organizing the data to make it suitable for machine learning.

4. **Modeling:** Building and evaluating machine learning models to solve the business problem.

5. **Evaluation:** Assessing the performance of the models in achieving the business objectives.

6. **Deployment:** Integrating the model into the production environment.

This neat, linear progression is a perfect fit for some of the data projects we previously described. In this context, a model is just a part of a pipeline, built to generate a particular report.

However, modern machine learning systems are much more akin to products than pipelines. They have many interconnected components and are applied to a much wider range of problems. On a basic technical level, they introduce several difficult challenges:

- **Data size and variety:** With the advent of big data, machine learning projects often involve massive datasets with diverse data types, such as text, images, and structured data. New approaches are needed to handle these different data sources.

- **Complex algorithms:** Machine learning algorithms have become more sophisticated, particularly with the emergence of deep learning, reinforcement learning, etc. These algorithms require specialized tools and frameworks for implementation and training.

- **Model deployment:** Modern machine learning systems require continuous model updates and monitoring, making deployment a complex, ongoing process.

- **Scalability:** Generating reports once a month is one thing, but performing real-time inference on demand for thousands of concurrent users is a massive challenge.

- **Collaboration:** Machine learning often involves a team of data scientists, data engineers, and domain experts. Collaboration tools and platforms have become essential to managing these cross-functional teams.

- **Ethical considerations and governance:** While not strictly a technical concern, the increasing impact of machine learning on society has made ethical concerns and governance practices a higher priority. Ensuring fairness, transparency, and compliance have become essential components of machine learning systems.

Luckily, some very talented data scientists and engineers have been working on these problems for years, and the modern ML ecosystem is full of tools that make these challenges significantly easier. We have solutions for data versioning, experiment tracking, and collaborating across teams. We have model registries, and tools for monitoring models in production. Data lakes and warehouses enable us to manage, store, and query large volumes of data effectively. Machine learning frameworks have made modeling so much easier. There are even open source libraries for ensuring ethical and responsible use of machine learning models.

Throughout this book, we'll explore all of these tools and actually build projects on top of them. But, before we go any deeper, we should take a moment to discuss perhaps the biggest shift in the machine learning ecosystem over the last decade: large language models.

The Emergence of LLMs Has Increased ML's Power and Complexity

Now, we turn our attention to one of the most transformative developments in the field of machine learning: the emergence of large language models (LLMs), which has significantly increased both the power and complexity of ML systems. Models like GPT-3, BERT, and their successors have redefined the limits of what's possible in natural language understanding and generation.

These models, characterized by their immense size and pretrained parameter estimates, have proven versatile and capable of various tasks. For example, LLMs have achieved unprecedented performance in natural language understanding (NLU) functions, such as sentiment analysis, text summarization, language translation, and question-answering. They have fundamentally changed the landscape of natural language processing (NLP). LLMs can generate coherent, context-aware text across diverse styles and domains and are the driving force behind the proliferation of content-generation tools, chatbots, and AI-assisted writing.

> A *pretrained* AI model has typically been trained on a large dataset to perform a certain task. The data can be of any type including images, text, audio, tabular data, etc, depending on the use case. They are typically state-of-the-art deep learning models.

In addition, pretrained LLMs have become powerful tools for transfer learning. By fine-tuning domain-specific data, these models

7

can be adapted to various applications, reducing the need for extensive labeled data with each new use case. They can even be applied to tasks involving modalities beyond text, such as images and audio. This convergence of modalities opens new avenues for complex, multimodal applications such as image captioning, visual question-answering, and more.

Increased capabilities, however, come with increased complexity. For example, consider the following common LLM tasks:

- **Language understanding:** LLMs can understand nuanced language and context, enabling more sophisticated and context-aware AI systems, such as chat agents. However, chat agents require frequent inference (i.e., the process of running inference with a trained AI model to make a prediction or solve a task). How can we handle 1,000 concurrent users, each requiring inference every few seconds, with a 17-billion parameter model?

- **Knowledge extraction:** LLMs can extract structured knowledge from unstructured text, which has broad applications in data mining, information retrieval, and content curation. But how do we ingest and store this knowledge? How do we make it possible for our system to even find it dynamically?

- **Content generation:** LLMs can generate content that is highly creative and contextually relevant, such as poetry, code, and even entire articles. This complexity extends to AI-generated art, music, and literature development. How do we generate content while ensuring that we respect copyright law? How do we protect against racism or otherwise toxic output? What about misinformation?

- **Multimodal AI:** Integrating LLMs with other deep learning models, such as convolutional neural network (CNNs) tasks like image processing, leads to complex, powerful multimodal

AI systems. These systems can understand and generate content that combines text, images, and other data types. However, all of these models must be deployed and managed in concert. How can we do this effectively?

Research and development efforts are making these models more efficient, interpretable, and less resource-intensive. As LLMs become more accessible, they have the potential to democratize AI and empower even more innovation in diverse fields.

Throughout this book, as we explore the new world of machine learning, we will use an LLM-focused project to demonstrate. For completeness, we'll also present examples along the way with tabular data.

What You Can Expect from This Book

This book is principally a guide to MLOps and LLMOps for data scientists from a more traditional BI-focused or research-heavy background. We will be building projects of our own using the tools and principles we explore throughout the following chapters. We hope you will use these techniques in your future projects. Broadly, we will cover the following:

- **Data pipeline and version control:** We will introduce the concept of data pipelines and version control for data preparation. This ensures that data is consistently processed and changes to the pipeline can be tracked and managed.
- **Experimentation and model versioning:** We will expand the modeling phase to include things such as architecture search and model versioning.
- **Continuous evaluation:** We will extend the evaluation phase to involve continuous model performance monitoring and

A Gentle Introduction to Modern Machine Learning

implement automated checks to detect performance degradation over time.

- **Continuous deployment:** We will update the deployment phase to include continuous deployment, enabling the rapid deployment of updated models. We never added A/B testing.

- **Monitoring and model retraining:** We will add a maintenance phase to monitor models in production, retraining our models on new data as needed.

- **Collaborative tools and workflow:** We will promote collaborative tools and workflows that facilitate cross-functional cooperation between data scientists, data engineers, and operations teams.

MLOps principles are essential to navigate the evolving landscape of data science and machine learning. The challenges we've discussed, from data versioning to model evaluation and deployment, highlight the need for a systematic and scalable approach. By incorporating data pipelines, version control, experimentation, continuous evaluation, and collaborative workflows into your projects, you'll enhance reproducibility and scalability and ensure that your models remain effective and adaptive over time.

As we've already discussed, we'll use an LLM-based project to demonstrate these principles. Our application will perform question-answering using YouTube videos as an external data source. In the next chapter, we'll look at the philosophy behind our project (and modern ML systems in general) before diving into our project in Chapter 3.

## Chapter 2

An End-to-End Approach

The focus of this book is on building end-to-end, production machine learning systems. With that in mind, we should begin by defining what these terms mean. We promise—this isn't just pedantry. Over the last 20 years, terms like *end-to-end* and *production* have been thrown around a lot in the world of data science, and depending on the time period, their definitions may vary wildly.

Imagine working on a business intelligence team at a shoe retailer in 2015, when working with data looked quite different than it does today. Your team is tasked with sales forecasting for the next quarter. What would your end-to-end system look like?

You begin by building your dataset. Being 2015, it's very likely that your company's data is a nightmare to access and ingest, but after considerable effort, your team is able to curate a clean dataset. Next, you focus on modeling. Your team will probably experiment with a variety of models, from ARIMA to random forests and maybe even gradient boosting (XGBoost embeddings was initially released in 2014, after all). After much tweaking and tuning, and ideally some robust validation, you finally have your model. Now, you can get to the business of predicting next quarter's sales and sharing your results. Sharing your results could mean many things here. You may have produced a dashboard for the chief revenue officer (CRO) or manually generated predictions each day using a tool like Statistical Package for Social Sciences (SPSS). Maybe you scheduled a job to run every day that would create the new day's actuals via a macro. Or you might start your day by inspecting the forecast and writing an email to share the results.

The hypothetical sales forecasting project is, in many ways, straightforward. This is not to say that it is *easy*. Any project that requires this much manual effort is difficult. Curating a dataset from years of unhygienic legacy data is arduous. Presenting your forecasts to a nontechnical audience without boring them is an art. There are a seemingly infinite number of experiments you might run in the modeling phase, and conducting a reliable validation process is rarely simple. But, if we break down the components of this project, there aren't that many architectural decisions to make.

- **Data ingestion:** How your company has stored its data will ultimately guide this, but you will need to decide how you are going to ingest data and produce a dataset.

- **ML framework:** In all likelihood, you will be using something like scikit-learn (a Python library for modeling) to build your model, but because it's 2015, you could also be using a statistical tool or some internal framework your team built.

- **Visualization library:** If your company uses a particular dashboarding solution, you'll use that. Otherwise, you'll use whatever library you like or Excel to generate charts for your report.

And that's basically it. You don't need to make more architectural decisions. Because it's 2015, you probably aren't using any real experiment management solution outside of a spreadsheet. Data versioning isn't likely to be done in any official sort of way. Your model doesn't need to be "deployed" in any sense, although if you're using a macro, that might technically qualify. You will probably generate predictions by running a notebook or a local script, which *might* be stored with some kind of version control. But generally speaking, this is all that is encompassed by your end-to-end system, and *it works*—at least, for this particular system.

But what about a more complex machine learning system, like the YouTube search assistant we mentioned in Chapter 1? This system requires multiple models interacting in a pipeline. It involves a database with support for vectors to store embeddings.

A *vector database* is a database built for storing and querying high-dimensional data. Many popular techniques like RAG (Retrieval Augmented Generation) rely on manipulating text embeddings, which are high dimensional vectors, stored in vector databases.

The application must implement some retrieval logic to get relevant videos and excerpts, a way to generate transcripts from videos, and create embeddings for that text. Your inference pipeline needs to be accessible for real-time generation, and your front end can't simply be a chart in some report—you need a full-blown application. And, of course, your system needs to be able to scale to handle many concurrent users.

Beyond any individual technical difference, the most important difference to note is that this system is not a one-off bit of data analysis. It is an ongoing software project, one that needs to be maintained, monitored, and, ideally, improved.

In this chapter, we are going to introduce a framework for designing such a machine learning system. We will begin by examining our YouTube search assistant in a bit more detail.

Components of a YouTube Search Agent

First, let's describe our system generally. When a user inputs their question, the system searches YouTube for relevant videos and adds

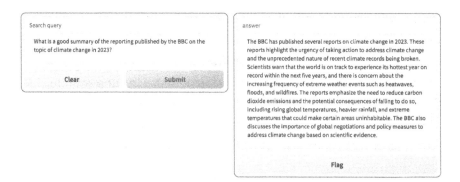

Figure 2.1 YouTube search query

their transcripts to our ever-growing database. Then, the system extracts the most relevant embeddings and associated text, based on an embedding created for the user's search query from our entire database, and the text is then passed to our language model. In practice, the end result is shown in Figure 2.1.

The model used here wasn't trained on data from 2023, so this is an example of using retrieval augmented generation (RAG) to share entirely new information with a language model. We'll talk more about RAG in a later chapter.

Let's think through the different components of this project. At a very high level, our components fit into a few discrete categories:

- **YouTube retrieval:** We have a system for running YouTube searches and fetching the relevant videos. We then generate transcripts from these videos.

- **Embeddings storage:** We use an embedding model to convert chunks of our transcripts into embeddings and then store them in a vector database. We then convert our user's initial question into an embedding, using the same embedding model, and performing a similarity search to retrieve the most relevant excerpts from our videos. Finally, we return the text associated with the embedding and input context for our final LLM inference.

- **Large language models:** Throughout our system, we use LLMs in key places. We use a model to convert our users' questions into relevant YouTube searches, to conduct our final question-answering task, and to generate our embeddings.

- **User interface:** We take user inputs and display outputs inside our application.

Within each of those categories, we have many individual components that need to be designed and implemented. In Figure 2.2, we've laid out a diagram of the major components.

It's important to understand how interdependent the different components in this system are. Your embeddings are only as good as the text you are embedding, which means your transcription system is essential. At the same time, a perfect transcription system is useless if you are unable to find relevant videos, which means your YouTube retrieval system must be great.

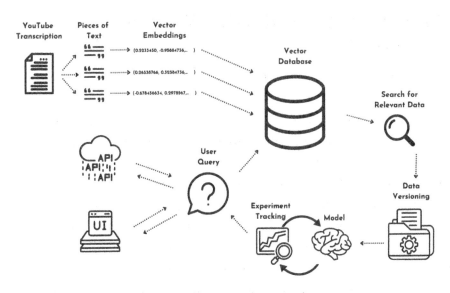

Figure 2.2 Components of a YouTube search

An End-to-End Approach

Many of your design decisions will be made for you, based on the needs of your project. For example, if you need to fine-tune your models, then the field of potential LLM architectures you might use will narrow considerably, as many of the most popular hosted APIs don't allow fine-tuning and many popular model architectures would be prohibitively expensive to fine-tune on your own. At the same time, many of the decisions regarding infrastructure in a system like this might not be at all obvious to you—at least, not until something breaks.

What does it take to handle many concurrent users in a system like this? If the quality of your system's outputs starts to deteriorate, how would you even know? And once you did know, where would you begin to debug? If you have an entire team of data scientists and engineers working on improving this application, how can you attribute a change in your application's outputs to a particular change in the system?

Principles of a Production Machine Learning System

Architecture is a tricky subject in software engineering—mostly because no one is really sure what it is. Loosely, people tend to say "architecture" when they are discussing the fundamental logic of a system separate from the actual code that implements it. Unsurprisingly, these discussions have a tendency toward pageantry, producing lots of diagrams, taxonomies, and "methodologies" that are promptly ignored by the people who actually build things.

However, this is not to say that architecture is an ignorable concept, just that it needs to be understood through a more practical lens. We quite like one particular definition of architecture from Ralph Johnson, shared by Martin Fowler: "Architecture is about the important stuff. Whatever that is."

In that spirit, we want to focus on what we consider "the important stuff" in designing a machine learning system. Our goal is not to outline a checklist or rigid methodology but rather to share a set of core principles to consider when designing your machine learning infrastructure with real code examples of how you might apply each.

Any production machine learning system needs to emphasize the following:

- **Observability:** When our system's outputs begin to degrade, we need to notice it, and we need to be able to work backwards to understand where the degradation is stemming from. This is more than monitoring, which involves recording and displaying data. Observability involves actual analysis of our system's internals. In the context of machine learning, this requires our models to have some level of *explainability*. We need to know, for example, what it looks like when our question-answering task is failing because of an upstream issue with our context generation, as opposed to when it is failing because the question is just too complex for the model to handle. Observability is invaluable for root-cause analysis.

- **Reproducibility:** Machine learning systems are inherently probabilistic, which can make it difficult to definitively say how a particular change affected the overall system; this also means that you can train the model on the same data and get different results. To be confident in any decision we make, we need to be able to reproduce our results, which means we need robust tracking and versioning of all the different parameters and pieces of internal state that comprise our system.

- **Interoperability:** Some people may not consider this a universal principle as much as it is our preference. After all, there are plenty of companies running on software stacks that are not interoperable outside of their ecosystem but are still robust and stable. In machine learning, however, where the field is changing so rapidly, interoperability is essential. You might want to be able to adopt some huge breakthrough the field generates, and having an interoperable platform makes this easier.

- **Scalability:** Scale is one of the defining problems of production machine learning. Even for simpler machine learning systems, handling thousands of concurrent users can often require huge amounts of computational resources. If your system isn't designed with this in mind, costs can easily spiral out of control (or your application can simply fail).

- **Improvability:** Your machine learning system must be built in such a way that it can be improved. This might sound silly and obvious, but it's not a given in machine learning projects. Take the sales forecasting example from the beginning of this chapter. After all the model fitting or parameter tuning and experimentation that went into squeezing the last bits of performance out of that model, how would you improve things? Would another data scientist be able to pick that project up six weeks later and meaningfully improve things without starting from scratch? Would they even be able to find the training code? The original creator probably tried all sorts of combinations of variables and different techniques, and the new modeler is most likely missing this context.

We would *really* like for that list to work out to a cool acronym that implied something about MLOps, but alas, extensive research has concluded that "orisi" is a Fijian surname, an Italian grape variety, and a word for people from the Indian state of Orissa. If any of those strike you as particularly relevant to software infrastructure, feel free to use the acronym, but we'll carry on without it.

To ground things a little more in reality, let's briefly look at how each of these principles applies to our YouTube system. We will go much further in depth for each of these components in later chapters, with actual coded examples, but for now this should give you a sense of what is to come.

Observability

Observability is a measure of how accurately we can estimate the internal state of our system from its external outputs. In other words, if we look at the total output of our system—not just the answers it generates, but any logs, alerts, or other analytics—how well can we understand what is happening inside the system?

Like most things in software engineering, observability is infinitely optimizable. In our projects throughout this book, we are going to do our best to strike a balance between implementing useful, production-ready observability and keeping the technical complexity reasonable for a single person.

For our YouTube search agent, our first crack at observability would be to use a tool like OpenLLMetry to automatically track our chain of interactions with our models. We would then have a traceable snapshot of how our model was behaving at each step of the process, including its prompts, responses, and metadata. From there, we could implement some basic alerting.

If we start getting lower quality answers from our system, with these observability features in place, we can actually look at the prompt and response for each stage of our workflow. We will often be able to immediately diagnose potential causes for deterioration from this data.

Reproducibility

Following our ideas around observability, let's imagine you've diagnosed a potential issue in the way your context window is constructed.

An End-to-End Approach

You implement a fix, and things seem to be working better. How can you be sure that you actually fixed the problem? Maybe there was something peculiar about the previous searches, something that hasn't cropped up in recent searches, and your "fix" didn't actually change anything.

To be sure, you need to be able to reproduce the exact searches that returned poor results. To do this, you will need access to the exact data, parameters, and prompts as the previous searches. Our parameters and prompts are preserved by our observability platform, but our data requires an additional tool.

We'll go deeper in the next chapter, but at a high level, we will use one of the many tools built for version controlling machine learning data. This will allow us to make sure that the same data is available to our system when we test our changes.

Interoperability

Any number of things could happen to make you want to change a component in this system. Maybe a new company releases a foundation model better than OpenAI's. Maybe you want to stand your own LLM up, or you develop a better system for searching videos. Whatever the case, the state of the art changes quickly in machine learning, and having a system that can adapt to these changes is important if you want to keep up.

Building interoperable software is a topic that goes beyond machine learning and could be the topic of many books. Instead of going deep into philosophies of software architecture, we are going to focus on some actionable principles for you to keep in mind. We'll flesh these out more in Chapter 5, "Putting Together an Application," but for now, the key idea is modularity.

When implementing our system, we want to contain every basic operation of our system inside its own atomic function. Each function and each tool is responsible for only one thing. In principle, this allows us to swap individual pieces out without cascading failures. For example, in a later chapter, we will write a `get_completion()` method for calling our LLMs. If we were to change foundation models, all we would have to do is edit this single function, and everything should work the same. Similarly, our observability platform can output data to any host, meaning we can change our analytics platform however we like without disrupting our system. Data interoperability is also a big challenge when getting models into production. Although we expect our phones and phone apps to have a high level of interoperability, with different devices and platforms communicating, sharing data, and working together seamlessly, it is often not the case in industry, particularly in healthcare. Often data sources across departments will come from different (sometimes legacy) systems, with different formats and structure. "Data silos" as they're often called, can be a huge hurdle in getting machine learning models into production.

Scalability

There are two main questions we want to answer with regard to scale: Can our system handle a large number of concurrent users, and can our system handle a large number of concurrent users *without exceeding our budget?*

To illustrate the importance of that second question, let's look at a real-world example. In late 2019, an ML researcher named Nick Walton shared an AI-powered dungeon crawler game he'd built by fine-tuning GPT-2. The game was playable via a Jupyter notebook, which was shared via Google Colab. At the time, Colab offered free GPUs for all users, so Nick believed this to be a free way to scale the game.

The game was amazing, and rightfully, it immediately went viral. Tens of thousands of people began playing it, all of whom were running Colab notebooks that downloaded a 5 GB model from Nick's storage. This data transfer was not free, so quickly, the cost of hosting this "free" game exceeded $10,000 per day. It was actually cheaper for Nick and his collaborators to launch the game as a full-blown application, with the model deployed to AWS.

Cloud computing has given everyone the compute resources necessary to run huge models, allowing companies to nearly bankrupt themselves running systems that are incredibly expensive to scale due to inference and training costs. In this YouTube search agent project, which we'll be implementing across the next several chapters, we've taken care to ensure our system scales in a manageable way. For example, our vector database runs on a Kubernetes cluster, allowing it to scale rapidly. For ease of use, we use the generous free hosted plan provided by Zilliz, its maintainer. At the same time, the database is open source. This means that if our system scaled so large that we exceeded the free plan, we could quickly calculate whether self-hosting the database would be a better financial decision. We've decoupled our system from any particular LLM for similar reasons. While we know that OpenAI's servers are unlikely to buckle under the traffic we send them, we also know that OpenAI's APIs aren't free, and sometimes OpenAI does things like oust its CEO without warning. If the cost were to increase past our budget, we could explore using cheaper models, or even hosting our own, without needing to refactor our entire system.

Improvability

There are two main ways we think about improvability as it relates to machine learning systems. The first is simple and shared with general software engineering: is our code written in such a way that we could easily refactor it to improve the system? This goes back to our points about interoperability and scalability. Any discrete improvement could be adopted into our system without massive disruption.

The second way we think about improvability is a bit more specific to machine learning (though it is also common to some other software projects, particularly those involving networks): does our system do a good job of improving itself?

This may seem vague at first, but think about our search pipeline. For a given query, our system will query only a limited number of new videos. However, once those videos are queried, they are entered into our vector database forever—and our similarity search is conducted against the *entire* database, not just the videos we most recently queried. So, the more people use our system, the more relevant videos we have stored in our database and the better our system will perform for future queries when users are using the same database. Through no intervention on our part, the system is improving itself.

This principle is especially relevant to systems that involve a retraining pipeline. In these kinds of systems, the more users provide feedback on a model's performance, the bigger the impact of the retraining pipeline.

A Note on Tools

Throughout this book, we will be using a lot of different third-party tools and libraries. There is no way around this, as implementing these tools from scratch would turn this book into a master's program. However, this does open the door to some potential issues. For example, what if a tool no longer exists by the time you read this book? Given the speed at which machine learning evolves, this seems likely.

To mitigate this, we've been careful to select tools that lend themselves to the principles of observability, reproducibility, interoperability, scalability, and improvability. In that spirit, here are a few notes on our criteria for choosing tools:

- We have selected no end-to-end platforms. There is no single tool that can make or break the projects you will build throughout this book.

- We have preferred open-source tools. Most of the tools we use here are open source, making it very likely that they are available by the time you read this book. Even in cases where we use cloud vendors, we've tried to work with vendors whose core product is open source (like Zilliz). We'll be using Comet for data versioning and experiment tracking. Although the core Comet product is not open source, it has a robust community edition and maintains many open-source projects.

- We have emphasized simple UIs. We have avoided tools that have highly idiomatic APIs or particular workflows. For example, our observability platform simply uses similar Python syntax to most other Python logging frameworks.

Now, with this high-level overview out of the way, we can start to dig into some actual projects.

Chapter 3

A Data-Centric View

Every data scientist knows that the quality of your dataset sets the bounds on the quality of your model. That's why we spend full days of our lives cleaning and wrangling messy data—and why data engineers, who automate much of this, deserve some sort of humanitarian award.

But historically, your dataset has been only one of the levers available to you as a data scientist. In a given machine learning project, the modeling phase would be equally important. You'd spend days experimenting with testing different learning algorithms and fitting parameters in your model to try to squeeze every last bit of r-squared or precision that you could. Although we still have uses for these algorithms, in many use cases we're now able to solve for, our approach is often different.

Things have changed. When constructing a modern machine learning system, increasing the quality and quantity of your data is the single most potent lever at your disposal. In this chapter, we'll dig into the factors that influenced this shift in the ML landscape and explore how it shapes the way we approach building ML systems.

The Emergence of Foundation Models

Perhaps the biggest contributor to the shift away from more model-centric focuses in machine learning is the widespread use of pretrained models, sometimes called *foundation models*. Trained on vast and diverse datasets, these models have a high baseline performance on many ML tasks, oftentimes higher than what we could possibly achieve with our dataset alone.

Leveraging pretrained models has drastically reduced the need for training models from scratch. In many cases, we still fine-tune the pretrained model with our own data, but the underlying model architecture has already been decided for us. At the risk of anthropomorphizing models, using a foundation model in this way is like hiring a data scientist and then teaching them about your domain, versus hiring a teenager and teaching them statistics, programming, data science, and your domain.

There are still plenty of data science projects where a simpler model is all you need, but for the kinds of systems we're focused on building in this book, pretrained foundation models are going to play a central role. These models, while hugely beneficial, bring their own unique challenges.

Many of the most popular foundation models are big. Enormous, in fact. GPT-3 cost $5 million for each training run, and hosting it requires roughly 350 GB of GPU memory.[1] This means that there is a roughly 0% chance of you hosting your own GPT-3 in the near future. The most realistic option for most people hoping to interact with these models is to use third-party, hosted APIs.

These APIs provide convenient access to various machine learning functionalities, from machine learning with tabular data and natural language processing tasks to computer vision. Integrating these APIs into your systems allows you to tap into cutting-edge ML

---

[1]Craig S. Smith, "What Large Language Models Cost You – There Is No Free AI Lunch", *Forbes*, September 8, 2023,: https://www.forbes.com/sites/craigsmith/2023/09/08/what-large-models-cost-you--there-is-no-free-ai-lunch/?sh=69ff51ed4af7

capabilities, increasingly becoming more domain-specific without starting from square one. Famous examples now are the OpenAI API and the Hugging Face Transformers API.

The difference between a pretrained model and an API is that a pretrained model is the model itself, often shared as model weights and architecture. In contrast, an API is a means of interacting with a model, typically hosted on a remote server, to perform specific tasks. You can use a pretrained model to build your applications, whereas an API allows you to make requests to an existing model hosted by a service provider. This allows you to build quickly, but it complicates issues around regulation and compliance and can make it harder to ensure your output is ethical.

The Role of Off-the-Shelf Components

In addition to pretrained models, the proliferation of off-the-shelf components for modern machine learning systems has shifted the field to a more data-centric view.

There is a lot of infrastructure involved in building a production machine learning system. You need a way to perform inference, whether you're running a monthly report or hosting a real-time inference API. And if you were part of a machine learning team in the mid-2010s, there's a good chance your company was building everything on their own, writing kernels in C++ and patching together their own model servers.

Building and maintaining all of this infrastructure was, for better or worse, partially the responsibility of the data science team—if not explicitly, at least ideally, as this work falls pretty clearly under the scope of engineering. But in reality, data scientists would be dedicating significant energy to working on or around their ML infrastructure. Now, this has all changed. For most pieces of ML infrastructure, the best-in-class solution is a ready-to-use component that can be installed or purchased and immediately plugged into your system.

These components include libraries, frameworks, and tools that streamline various aspects of the ML pipeline, from data preprocessing to model deployment. An example of an off-the-shelf component would be scikit-learn; it contains tools for data preprocessing, feature selection, model selection, and evaluation.

The ability to leverage off-the-shelf components, pretrained models, and APIs leaves one piece of the ML system entirely in the hands of the data scientist—the data itself.

The Data-Driven Approach

Fundamentally, a data-driven approach underpins the construction of modern ML systems. The biggest driver of quality in your system isn't going to be the model architecture you select or how efficiently you implement backpropagation; it will be how good your dataset is.

Consequently, the data acquisition and management process requires careful consideration, as the quality of your data directly impacts the performance and reliability of your ML system. A unique dataset is also your moat when building a product on top of your ML system. If you simply write a wrapper around a third-party API, it's not particularly difficult for another company to replicate your entire product—just ask any of the companies that built wrappers around OpenAI's API, only to be swallowed up by OpenAI's next product launch. What bigger competitors cannot replicate is your proprietary data.

By understanding the significance of data as your primary point of control in this process, you will be better equipped to navigate the complexities of the modern machine learning landscape.

A Note on Data Ethics

A chapter centered around data requires a note on data bias and ethics. Data is often inherently biased because people are biased.

People generate a lot of data, or at the very least, have a hand in collecting the data. Therefore, our models can produce biased, incorrect, or even dangerous results.

What we often call "bias" has many different meanings in data. In this context, we're discussing fairness in our data. Data used for training algorithms can inadvertently perpetuate different gender, racial, age, and socioeconomic biases. These biases arise from historical and societal inequalities, reflecting discriminative practices and stereotypes in data sources. When training machine learning models, the algorithms learn and reinforce these biases already in the data, leading to discriminatory outcomes. You'll want to assess your data for bias during the data preparation phase, but you'll also want to keep a close eye on and evaluate the data output from the model.

For example, there have been articles about companies attempting to use "biased hiring algorithms." But it's not the algorithm *exactly* that was biased; it's the underlying data. Biased hiring data might result in algorithms favoring certain genders, ages, or races, perpetuating inequitable practices in hiring. You need to ensure that your model is not producing biased results, like penalizing a Black-sounding name or being a graduate of a women's college, and that means curating a dataset that doesn't implicitly represent white men as de facto "winning candidates."

Another recent example comes from the realm of generative AI, where an Asian woman leveraged an image generation tool to create a "professional" photo. In all the returned headshots, the tool portrayed her as white, because its dataset had led it to associate whiteness with professionalism.[2]

---

[2]Sawdah Bhaimiya, "An Asian MIT Student Asked AI To Turn An Image of Her Into a Professional Headshot. It Made Her White, With Lighter Skin and Blue Eyes", *Business Insider*, August 1, 2023: Asian woman gets white professional photos: `https://www.businessinsider.com/student-uses-playrgound-ai-for-professional-headshot-turned-white-2023-8`

A Data-Centric View

Recognizing and addressing these biases is critical for creating fair and inclusive machine learning systems. All training data will inherently contain bias, but it's crucial to ensure that the application of the model will not cause harm due to discrimination. Collaborating with domain experts and involving diverse perspectives in the evaluation process, in addition to your eye, can provide valuable insights to mitigate potential bias. Analysis before creating a model and monitoring and evaluating the output can help you identify these cases.

The goal is to inform you of the biases you'll encounter, allowing you to avoid risks and promote responsible adoption. If you'd like to read more deeply about biased data and the impact it can have, we highly recommend reading Cathy O'Neil's book *Weapons of Math Destruction* (Crown, 2017).

Building the Dataset

Let's get started building our own dataset. In a later section, we'll implement a pipeline for fetching new YouTube video transcripts, but we'll start with a static collection of transcripts from well-known data science YouTubers. I've taken the transcriptions from 16 different videos. These include videos from Josh Starmer (StatQuest), Ken Jee, Kate Strachnyi (DATAcated), and myself (Kristen Kehrer—although I have yet to become a well-known YouTuber). I used the *Pytube* library to load the transcriptions, including the associated metadata. The metadata we're interested in keeping for this project is the title and author of the video. Code examples in this book are here:

```
https://github.com/machine-learning-upgrade
```

To see what the original transcription looks like, we'll first pip install (package installer for Python) LangChain. Then, we'll pass the URL to the `YoutubeLoader` and load the transcription. This code snippet came directly from the LangChain documentation:

https://python.langchain.com/docs/integrations/
document_loaders/youtube_transcript

To get the transcription from a single YouTube video, use this:

```
!pip install youtube-transcript-api==0.6.1 langchain
==0.0.335 pytube==15.0.0

from langchain.document_loaders import YoutubeLoader

loader = YoutubeLoader.from_youtube_url(
    "https://www.youtube.com/watch?v=Q4OBx3S0Ysw
&t=118s", add_video_info=True
)


data = loader.load()
data[0].page_content
```

Now, you should be able to see the transcription of any You-Tube video you pass to it, along with the metadata. The output shows the transcription, title, author, view count, publish date, time, and length. You'll be interested in returning the relevant text, title, and author. This way, you can find the particular video with the information you're interested in. To do this, you'll need to store these transcripts in a database.

The choice between a vector, graph, or relational database for text data depends on your specific use case. Vector databases are a great choice when semantic understanding and similarity search are vital, especially for high-dimensional text data. Your cloud provider probably also offers database options that include functionality for working with vector embeddings. Opt for a graph database if you're capturing complex relationships and performing network analysis or if your data has a natural graph structure. Choose a relational data-base for structured text data with defined relationships.

Since we leverage our text data for an LLM use case and care about the semantic understanding of our output, we'll use a vector database. This data will be going into a vector database for our project, but first, we need to do some processing. As it stands now, if we were to create an embedding for this, the whole transcription text would be in one vector embedding. To search the text at the granularity we want, we can't compress 15 minutes of text content into one embedding! The answer is to chunk the text into smaller excerpts.

Although you could write a program to take the text and split it rudimentarily by creating text chunks of a certain number of characters or by creating a vector simply for each sentence, LangChain has a text splitter that works smarter than that. The following is from the LangChain documentation (`https://js.langchain.com/docs/modules/data_connection/document_transformers/`):

At a high level, text splitters work as follows:

- Split the text into small, semantically meaningful chunks.
- Start combining these small chunks into a larger chunk until you reach a certain size (as measured by some function).
- Once you reach that size, make that chunk its own piece of text and then start creating a new chunk with some overlap (to keep context between chunks).

That means there are two different axes along which you can customize your text splitter:

- How the text is split.
- How the chunk size is measured.

The text splitter allows you to specify the maximum number of characters before each split with the chunk_size by how many characters the text chunks can overlap with the chunk_overlap variable. The length_function here is the built-in Python function that calculates the length of a string. add_start_index=True means that each chunk will have an index. An index helps track the position of each piece from the original text, which is what you want.

```
from langchain.text_splitter import
RecursiveCharacterTextSplitter
text_splitter = RecursiveCharacterTextSplitter(
  chunk_size = 1000,
  chunk_overlap = 50,
  length_function = len,
  add_start_index = True,
)

texts = text_splitter.create_documents([data[0].
page_content])

## Inspect the different pieces of text
print(texts[0])
print(texts[1])
print(texts[2])
```

Now, you have your text in smaller parts. Each text string needs to be transformed into a vector. To do this, you'll choose a machine learning algorithm to create your embeddings.

Working with Vector Databases

When using a vector database, you'll need to pick an index, a method for creating embeddings (this is where you are currently), and a distance measure to calculate how similar these vectors are.

When you select an index, you're typically making a trade-off between three different factors: speed, memory, and accuracy. Depending on your needs, you could optimize for any of these factors. For example, you'll have less accuracy with a quantized index, but it's small and fast.

There are different types of indexes.

- **Tree-based indexes:** Tree-based indexes employ binary search trees to search high-dimensional spaces swiftly. They structure the tree to group similar data points in the same subtree for faster searches in high-dimensional spaces. However, tree-based indexes excel in low-dimensional data but struggle to represent high-dimensional data accurately due to their inability to capture data complexity. An example is Approximate Nearest Neighbors Oh Yeah (ANNOY) by Spotify.

- **Graph-based indexes:** Graph-based indexes represent data points in a graph where nodes are data values, and edges symbolize their similarity. These indexes connect similar data points with efficient Approximate Nearest Neighbor (ANN) search algorithms, making them adept at finding approximate nearest neighbors in high-dimensional data while saving memory. An example is Hierarchical Navigable Small World (HNSW).

- **Hash-based indexes:** Reduces high-dimensional data to lower-dimensional hash codes, preserving original similarity. The dataset is hashed multiple times during indexing to increase collisions among similar points, in contrast to conventional hashing. Query points are hashed using the same functions, enabling rapid retrieval from the same hash bucket. These indexes offer speed for large datasets but sacrifice accuracy. An example is Locally Sensitive Hashing (LSH).

- **Quantization-based indexes:** Quantized indexes blend existing indexes (IVF, HNSW, Vamana) with compression techniques like quantization to trim memory usage and hasten searches. Two common quantization methods are Scalar Quantization (SQ) and Product Quantization (PQ).

Next, you create vector embeddings from this data. Vector embeddings (arrays of real numbers) allow your model to capture the semantic meaning. A machine learning model creates the embeddings, and the encoding will enable you to write a query and find the most semantically similar vectors to then use that information to pass to the model.

Text Embedding

Embeddings allow you to measure how related two text strings are. Embeddings can be leveraged for use cases such as search, classification, recommendations, clustering, detecting anomalies, and diversity measurement.

Selecting an algorithm for text embeddings looks quite different from how we've historically chosen an algorithm for structured data. Deep learning models have traditionally been differentiated based on their architecture, but these new models are often chosen based on the parameter count and the data used for training.

For example, finding a model that uses healthcare data in training might make sense if you're using your data for a healthcare use case.

Hugging Face leverages model cards to help provide this information about the model. You can choose the type of task you're doing, libraries you plan on leveraging, datasets for training, languages, and licenses. There are currently more than 1,300 models on Hugging

Face for NLP summarization, but after making your selections, you can sort by "most downloads" or "most likes" and read further about the model on the site.

> Hugging Face is a startup that maintains Transformers, the popular Python library for working with language models, as well as a hub for hosting and sharing datasets, models, and inference APIs.

You will use Zilliz as your vector database to create these embeddings. Zilliz is the perfect choice because it is cloud-based and managed Milvus. Milvus is a free, open-source, robust vector database designed to store, index, and handle massive embedding vectors generated by deep neural networks and other machine learning models. There are several vector databases, and the one you use will depend on your needs. Most cloud providers will also offer either a vector database or a database with functionality for working with vector embeddings. Figure 3.1 shows the options in Azure from `https://learn.microsoft.com/en-us/azure/cosmos-db/vector-database`.

The following comparison data was provided by Yujian Tang, senior developer advocate at Zilliz.

	Description
Azure Cosmos DB for Mongo DB vCore	Store your application data and vector embeddings together in a single MongoDB-compatible service featuring native support for vector search.
Azure Cosmos DB for PostgreSQL	Store your data and vectors together in a scalable PostgreSQL offering with native support for vector search.
Azure Cosmos DB for NoSQL with Azure AI Search	Augment your Azure Cosmos DB data with semantic and vector search capabilities of Azure AI Search.

Figure 3.1 Vector database options in Azure

A Comparison of Existing Open-Source Technologies (2024)

These are open-source, purpose-built engines to searches. The reason we do not comment on closed source is because the information is often unavailable. Figure 3.2, Figure 3.3, and Figure 3.4 show the various attributes for common vector databases.

	Separation of storage and compute	Separation of query and insertions	Multiple Replicas	Data Sharding	Cloud Native	Tested at Billion Scale
Milvus	Yes	Yes	Yes	Dynamic	Yes	Yes
Chroma	No	No	No	None	No	No
Qdrant	No	No	Yes	Static	Yes	Yes
Weaviate	No	No	Yes	Static	Yes	No
Zilliz	Yes	Yes	Yes	Yes	Yes	Yes

Figure 3.2 Scalability concerns

	Role-Based Access Control	Disk Index Support	Metadata Filtering	Partitions	Multi Vector Search	Number of Indexes
Milvus	Yes	Yes	Yes	Yes	Coming	11
Chroma	No	No	Yes	No	No	1
Qdrant	No	Yes	No	No	Yes	1
Weaviate	Coming	Yes	No	No	Yes	1
Zilliz	Yes	Yes	Yes	Yes	Coming	Automated

Figure 3.3 Functionality

Then, you need your distance metric. Although there are many distance metrics, these are the three common ones:

- **L2:** This is the Euclidean distance. L2 measures the distance between two vectors. A zero value means the vectors are identical and values can range from zero to infinity.

- **Cosine similarity:** This measures the cosine of the angle between two vectors. This measure does not take into consideration the magnitude of the vectors. Cosine similarity ranges between –1 and 1. A value of 1 means that two vectors are proportional, 0 means that the vectors are orthogonal, and –1 means that the vectors are opposites. If two vectors are further apart by Euclidean distance, there could still be a relatively small angle between the two vectors.

- **Inner product:** This measures distance and angle (orientation) between two vectors. If the vectors are L2 normalized, the inner product and cosine similarity are the same.

Armed with an understanding of indexes, embeddings, and distance metrics, you will load your data into a vector database.

	Purpose Built	Tunable Consistency	Stream and Batch Support	Binary Vector Support	SDK Languages
Milvus	Yes	Yes	Yes	Yes	Python Go Node C++ Ruby
Chroma	Yes	No	No	No	Python JavaScript
Qdrant	Yes	No	No	No	Python Go Rust
Weaviate	Yes	Yes	Yes	Yes	Python Go Java
Zilliz	Yes	Yes	Yes	Yes	Python Go Node C++ Ruby

Figure 3.4   Features beyond vector search

Getting Started with Zilliz

The Google Colab notebook with all of this code is in the Machine Learning Upgrade GitHub in the `book_code` repository if you want to follow along.

First, we demonstrate the creation of a Milvus collection, schema definition, and index setup using YouTube URLs that have been hard-coded. In the next chapter, the app will fetch YouTube videos for searches relevant to your query/use case.

Here is the high-level overview for the code:

- **Milvus setup:** The script begins by importing essential modules from PyMilvus and defining constants such as the collection name, embedding dimension, Zilliz cluster URI, and API key.

- **Connection:** It connects to the Zilliz cluster using the provided URI and API key.

- **Collection handling:** The script checks for any existing collection with the same name and drops it if found.

- **Schema definition:** It defines the fields for the collection, including video metadata (ID, title, author, etc.) and the embedding vector.

- **Collection creation:** A Milvus collection named `youtube` is created using the defined schema.

- **Index creation:** An index is created for the embedding field using the AUTOINDEX type and the Inner Product (IP) metric.

Before we dive in, you'll need an API key for both Zilliz and OpenAI. You'll want to go to `https://zilliz.com`, click Log In, and then click Sign Up. In the top navigation menu, you'll see API Keys, and you can click the + API Key button to create a new key.

To create an OpenAI key, you'll go to `https://openai.com`. In the top navigation, you'll see an API drop-down. If you choose

Overview from this drop-down, you can then click Get Started in the middle of the page, and you'll have the opportunity to create an account. Once your account is created, if you hover over the OpenAI logo in the top-left corner, that drop-down has an API Keys option. After clicking this, you'll have the ability to create your API key.

This data is going to be in JSON format. There's a chance that if your career has previously been spent working exclusively with tabular data, you're unfamiliar with the JSON format. JavaScript Object Notation (JSON) can open new avenues of flexibility and efficiency in handling diverse and nested data structures. JSON is a lightweight and human-readable data interchange format widely used for data storage and exchange on the Web.

Here are some benefits and uses of JSON for a data scientist:

- **Nested and flexible structure:** JSON allows for nested structures, making it adaptable to complex data relationships. This flexibility is especially noticeable when dealing with hierarchical or nested data. JSON is well-suited to representing semi-structured or unstructured data, like nested data in social media posts, log files, or responses from APIs.

- **Data interchange with APIs:** JSON is a standard format for data exchange between web services. Many APIs return data in JSON format.

- **Simplified data exploration and transformation:** JSON's human-readable format simplifies data exploration and transformation. Data scientists can easily inspect the data structure and adjust without requiring specialized tools.

- **Handling semistructured data:** JSON is ideal for representing semistructured data where not all records have the same fields. This is common in web scraping or dealing with variable data structures.

- **Compatibility with NoSQL databases:** Many NoSQL databases, such as MongoDB, use JSON-like structures to store data. Understanding JSON facilitates seamless interaction with these databases, enabling data scientists to work with a broader range of data storage solutions.

We start with installing our dependencies, and then you'll need to restart the runtime. You can restart the runtime by clicking Runtime at the top of your Google Colab and then clicking "Restart Session".

```
!pip install \
  pymilvus==2.3.4 \
  langchain==0.0.352 \
  openai==1.6.1 \
  pytube==15.0.0 \
  youtube-transcript-api==0.6.1 \
  pyarrow==14.0.2 \
  typing_extensions==4.9.0 \
  comet-ml==3.35.5

# Restart the runtime after pip installing (CTRL + M)
# Otherwise, the runtime remembers the old version of
# pyArrow and causes issues for pyMilvus
```

Now we'll import some libraries from Pymilvus that will allow us to connect to the database and create our collection and schema. In the code, we'll be defining our variables, setting up a list of YouTube URLs, creating a connection to the Zilliz cluster, creating the collection, and setting an index for the collection.

```python
from pymilvus import (MilvusClient
                      , connections
                      , Collection
                      , CollectionSchema
                      , FieldSchema
                      , DataType
                      , utility)
import json

COLLECTION_NAME = 'youtube'
EMBEDDING_DIMENSION = 1536  # Embedding vector size in
this example
ZILLIZ_CLUSTER_URI = 'YOUR ZILLIZ URI# Endpoint URI
obtained from Zilliz Cloud
ZILLIZ_API_KEY = 'YOUR ZILLIZ API KEY'

YT_VIDEO_URLS = [
    "https://www.youtube.com/
watch?v=Q4OBx3S0Ysw&t=118s",
    "https://youtu.be/4OZip0cgOho?si=KHUsA4
J8L3rbZAAZ"]

# Connect to the zilliz cluster
connections.connect(uri=ZILLIZ_CLUSTER_URI,
token=ZILLIZ_API_KEY, secure=True)

client = MilvusClient(
    uri=ZILLIZ_CLUSTER_URI,
    token=ZILLIZ_API_KEY)

# Remove any previous collections with the same name
if utility.has_collection(COLLECTION_NAME):
    utility.drop_collection(COLLECTION_NAME)
```

```python
# Create collection which includes the id, title, and
embedding.
fields = [
  FieldSchema(name='id', dtype=DataType.VARCHAR, is_
primary=True, auto_id=False, max_length=36),
  FieldSchema(name='video_id', dtype=DataType.INT64,),
  FieldSchema(name='title', dtype=DataType.VARCHAR,
description='Title texts', max_length=500),
  FieldSchema(name='author', dtype=DataType.VARCHAR,
description='Author', max_length=200),
  FieldSchema(name='part_id', dtype=DataType.INT64),
  FieldSchema(name='max_part_id',
dtype=DataType.INT64),
  FieldSchema(name='text', dtype=DataType.VARCHAR,
description='Text of chunk', max_length=2000),
  FieldSchema(name='embedding', dtype=DataType.FLOAT_
VECTOR, description='Embedding vectors',
dim=EMBEDDING_DIMENSION)
]

schema = CollectionSchema(fields=fields)

collection = Collection(name=COLLECTION_NAME,
schema=schema)

# Create an index for the collection.
index_params = {
    'index_type': 'AUTOINDEX',
    'metric_type': 'IP',
    'params': {}
}

collection.create_index(field_name="embedding",
index_params=index_params)
```

43

Next, we'll use the text splitter to break this text into chunks, and we'll use the text-embedding-ada-002 model by OpenAI to create our embeddings. Later, we'll load this data into the database. Other popular embedding models include Babbage, Curie, and Davinci. Notice that the EMBEDDING_DIMENSION from the previous code was set to 1536 dimensions; this is one-eighth the size of the davinci-001 embeddings model, meaning this is more cost-effective when working with vector databases.

```
from langchain.text_splitter import
RecursiveCharacterTextSplitter
import openai
from openai import OpenAI
from pymilvus import MilvusClient, connections
from uuid import uuid4
from langchain.document_loaders import YoutubeLoader
import youtube_transcript_api
import pytube


connections.connect(uri=ZILLIZ_CLUSTER_URI,
token=ZILLIZ_API_KEY, secure=True)

client = MilvusClient(
    uri=ZILLIZ_CLUSTER_URI,
    token=ZILLIZ_API_KEY)

openai_client = OpenAI(
    # defaults to os.environ.get("OPENAI_API_KEY")
    api_key="YOUR OPENAI API KEY",
)


# Extract embedding from text using OpenAI
string -> vector
```

```python
# This function is directly from https://docs.zilliz.
# com/docs/similarity-search-with-zilliz-cloud-and-
# openai, but with "text-embedding-ada-002" added.
def create_embedding_from_string(text):
    return openai_client.embeddings.create(
        input=text,
        model='text-embedding-ada-002').data[0].
embedding

text_splitter = RecursiveCharacterTextSplitter(
  chunk_size = 1000,
  chunk_overlap  = 50,
  length_function = len,
  add_start_index = True,
)

for video_id, url in enumerate(YT_VIDEO_URLS):

  yt_data = YoutubeLoader.from_youtube_url(url, add_
video_info=True).load()[0]
  video_parts = text_splitter.create_documents([yt_
data.page_content])

  for part_id, part in enumerate(video_parts):
      id = str(uuid4())
      print(f'uplading document {id}... {yt_data.
metadata["title"]}')
      client.insert(
        collection_name=COLLECTION_NAME,
        data={
            'id': id,
            'video_id': video_id,
            'title': yt_data.metadata['title'],
            'author': yt_data.metadata['author'],
```

```
        'part_id': part_id,
        'max_part_id': len(video_parts),
        'text': part.page_content,
        'embedding': create_embedding_from_
string(part.page_content)
        })
```

You'll insert the data into the collection. After insertion, you'll want to find the cluster to navigate to the YouTube collection on the Zilliz website.

To do this from `https://cloud.zilliz.com/orgs`, click Content Creation, as shown in Figure 3.5.

Then click your project (Figure 3.6).

Figure 3.5 Click Content Creation

Figure 3.6 Creating a project

Next choose the machine-learning-upgrade cluster (see Figure 3.7).

Then click youtube (see Figure 3.8).

Then you'll find a Data Preview tab, as shown in Figure 3.9.

As shown in Figure 3.10, you'll see a Load Collection button on the right.

Then click Load Data. Having to click a button to load the data manually is a nice feature so you're not duplicating your data if

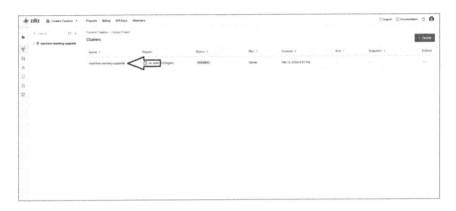

Figure 3.7   machine-learning-upgrade cluster

Figure 3.8   Connecting youtube

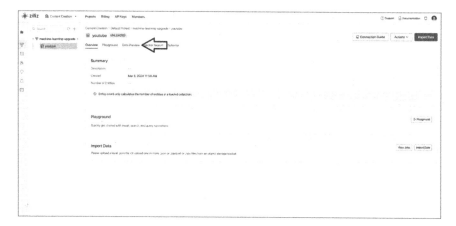

Figure 3.9 Data Preview tab

Figure 3.10 Load Collection button to preview data

you rerun a cell. You'll also need to grab an API key from OpenAI for this next bit of code, as shown in Figure 3.11.

We've got our embeddings, and our data is stored in a vector database. The next step is to create our data artifact. We will set up a data artifact using the whole dataset. If we weren't using the whole dataset for our query, an embedding would be created for the query, and then the distance metric chosen would be used to find the most

Figure 3.11 Viewing YouTube data with Zilliz

semantically similar vectors. To get at the total dataset, I've queried for the data from videos with `title = "none"`. It is possible to add a video to YouTube without a title, so this example does not scale, but this works for our purposes of creating a data artifact.

To query for all embeddings and the metadata, we'd like to track and store it as JSON like this:

```
results = collection.query(
    expr='title != "none"',
    output_fields=['title', 'author', 'part_id', 'max_
part_id', 'text'])
with open('data.json', 'w') as file:
  file.write(json.dumps(results, indent=2))
```

Once the data is finally in a usable state, you need to version control it, generating a data artifact so that you can reproduce your results later.

A Data-Centric View

Data Versioning and Management

Whenever you gather data for a new project, you need to implement data versioning. To use an example from Kristen's own life, one of my first computer vision projects was a simple (or so I thought) personal project for detecting my child's school bus as it approached our house. The bus has to pass my home and turn around before picking up my kids, so if my system could send me a text when it first saw the bus, I would get a five-minute heads up before my kids needed to be out the door. Wonderful!

To build my dataset, I took a video of the bus passing on my phone, turned the footage into image frames, and then annotated the images. The model didn't perform well, so I kept exploring.

Next, I downloaded pictures of buses from the Internet. I later learned that this would introduce colors, orientations, and other information into the model that my model would never see. It resulted in another unsuccessful model.

For my third attempt, I used the frames from the actual camera that would be doing the daily detection to create my training data. This third data set was the winner. I now had a successful dataset, but my data was now stored across multiple folders alongside the losing datasets. This didn't matter much in the short term—I knew which photos were the right ones, but in the long term, it burned me. When my kids went on summer vacation, I put the project down. Two months later, when they started school again, I decided to pick the project up, and at this point, I had no idea where the correct data lived.

Setting up the data for your project correctly from the beginning will help you avoid losing hours later trying to figure out which version of data trained the model. Since machine learning and AI are very iterative, your dataset often undergoes multiple iterations. You may add new features, find a new way to manipulate your data, or find new relevant data to include. All assets leveraged for the project need tracking and documentation, starting with the data.

More broadly, the benefits of data versioning include the following:

- **Traceability:** Track and understand the changes made to your data over time. This is especially important for compliance, auditing, and debugging in highly regulated industries.

- **Reproducibility:** By tracking previous versions of data, you're set up to reproduce your results. This ensures consistency and accuracy in research and builds trust in decision-making.

- **Collaboration:** Multiple users can work on and access the same dataset and find the correct version to reproduce results.

- **Data Recovery:** In case of mistakes or data corruption, data versioning provides a backup of previous versions.

Versioning data, however, is not easy. For example, Git is widely known as the most popular tool for versioning code. It efficiently tracks code changes, enables collaboration, and maintains a history of your codebase. However, when it comes to versioning data, Git's limitations become apparent. Large datasets can quickly bloat your repository, making it cumbersome. Additionally, Git doesn't provide native support for tracking changes within data files. However, Git LFS (Large File Storage) is built for managing large files with Git.

This is where specialized data versioning tools step in. With a data management tool, you can effortlessly version your datasets and track your data lineage while keeping your Git repository light-weight. The terms *lineage* and *artifact* are defined here since the terms get used somewhat loosely in conversations around data.

- **Data artifact:** This is a broad term. A data artifact is a collection of data you're storing. This could be your training set; metadata such as parameters, hyperparameters, source code, logs, and dependencies can all be data artifacts.

- **Data lineage:** This works as a map to show you where your data originated, how it changed through the life cycle, and where it's used, like for training a model or for a model in your model registry.

Data versioning functionality allows you to associate a specific dataset version with your experiments, and tracking the data lineage helps you understand how your data has changed over time. You can link a dataset version to a model training run, allowing you to more easily investigate differences and do rootcause analysis, like "Hey, what caused the difference in accuracy between these two models? Oh, that's right, we added more data before this training run."

Figure 3.12 shows what tracking data lineage looks like. You can see which data was used for a particular model run. The data is an artifact, although there are other types of artifacts. In the following data lineage example, one of the artifacts was a .pkl (pickle file). Pickle files are specific to Python and are a serialized binary

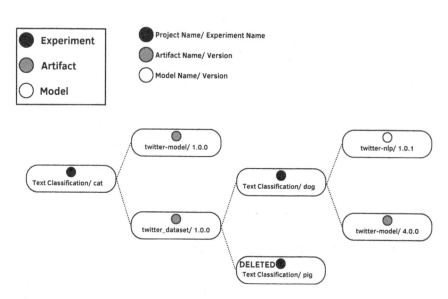

Figure 3.12 Data lineage model

representation of a Python object. Experiments are different training runs of a model. You can see the training runs and the data involved. The model in Figure 3.12 is the experiment training run added to the model registry. Typically, you move a model to the registry once you've decided that your final model will be placed in production.

You'll notice that although one of the training runs was deleted, you still have a record that it was deleted. The names "cat," "dog," and "pig" are made up. In an experiment tracking tool, the names of each run are randomly generated and assigned, but you can rename your models.

With data versioning, different team members can access and work with identical data versions, ensuring consistency and reducing the chances of confusion. It's like CliffsNotes for the project. Collaboration is another crucial piece to the success of data projects. Team members often find new roles or go on vacation, or plenty of projects are large enough that you're working on them as a team. This collaborative environment streamlines teamwork and eliminates the risk that a teammate will put in their two weeks in the middle of a project, leaving you stranded.

Tools like Comet, DVC, and others for data versioning bridge this gap, empowering data professionals to version their datasets, ensure reproducibility, and collaborate seamlessly. Leveraging specialized data versioning tools sets the foundation for more robust and efficient data workflows.

Getting Started with Data Versioning

We will use Comet's community version to illustrate data versioning. Leveraging a data versioning solution enables us to seamlessly keep track of any data associated with the ML life cycle. We both previously worked for Comet, making the tool an obvious choice for us. In the current machine learning landscape, it's important to note the tool itself is not as important as achieving the tenets outlined in this book. Data Version Control (DVC) is another popular choice for data versioning and management and is open source.

First, you'll create an account with Comet and get your API key to follow along. You can reference the quick-start guide here:

`https://www.comet.com/docs/v2/guides/getting-started/quickstart`

To find your Comet API key, click your username in the top-right corner of the site at `https://comet.com`. Then choose Account Setting from the drop-down, and you'll see API Keys as an option on the right side of the Account Settings page.

```
## First, we'll pip install the Comet library
!pip install comet_ml

## import comet_ml
from comet_ml import Experiment

## Create an experiment with your api key
experiment = Experiment(
    api_key='[YOUR_COMET_API_KEY]',
    project_name='youtube_transcriptions',
    workspace='[YOUR_COMET_USERNAME]'
)
```

Running this code, with nothing else, you'll be able to see that you've now set up a project named `youtube_transcriptions` by clicking the Comet logo in the top-left corner. It will count this as an experiment run, but there won't be anything in there, since you haven't done anything. When you start tracking your model runs, having this experiment function at the top of your code will automatically track everything associated with the model as long as Comet integrates with the framework (see Figure 3.13).

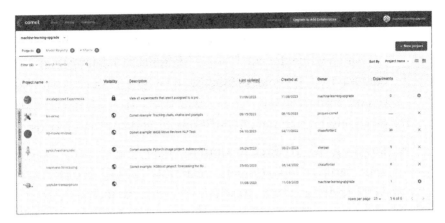

Figure 3.13 Comet dashboard

The Comet project page should show zero artifacts near the top-left corner. You're about to add your first artifact. Artifacts are vital to maintaining data lineage and ensuring a clear understanding of the data used in your machine learning experiments. These artifacts will live in the Comet Workspace level and are identified by unique names. They offer the flexibility to manage multiple versions of your data, providing a detailed history of your datasets and their evolution.

Adding an artifact is done in three steps. Here, we're paraphrasing the Comet Python SKD:

```
https://www.comet.com/docs/v2/api-and-sdk/
python-sdk/artifacts-overview/#:~:text=To%20log
%20an%20Artifact%2C%20you,Comet%20through%20the
%20Experiment%20object
```

1. **Create an artifact version:** You'll create an artifact instance and specify the version number, aliases, metadata, and version tags. Comet will auto-increment to the next major version if you don't specify a version number.

2. **Add files and folders:** It's time to populate your artifact version with files and folders called *artifact assets*. These assets

can be classified into artifact assets and remote artifact assets. The former includes files and folders with content uploaded to Comet, while the latter stores references to data without the content itself. If you're dealing with GCS or S3 bucket paths as remote artifact assets, Comet will keep track of all the files, providing lineage benefits without additional data uploads.

3. **Logging the artifact to Comet:** When you're ready to send your artifact to Comet, use the `experiment.log_artifact(artifact)` method to finalize the process.

To add your artifact, you may need to rerun previous cells in Google Colab, but there you'll run this:

```
artifact = Artifact(name="milvus-query-results", artifact_type="dataset")

artifact.add("data.json")

experiment.log_artifact(artifact)
experiment.end()
```

Now, you have your data stored as an artifact, as shown in Figure 3.14. You can see here that I've run this several times and that the versions are automatically managed.

If you click the latest version, you'll have the option to click and see the metadata or lineage; if you click the file, you'll see a preview of your data in JSON format. Congratulations! You've just created your first data artifact (see Figure 3.15).

As shown in Figure 3.16, if you click `data.json`, you'll see the JSON that is stored.

These artifacts form the foundation for your ML-driven endeavor. In industry, it takes much more than grabbing a couple of YouTube

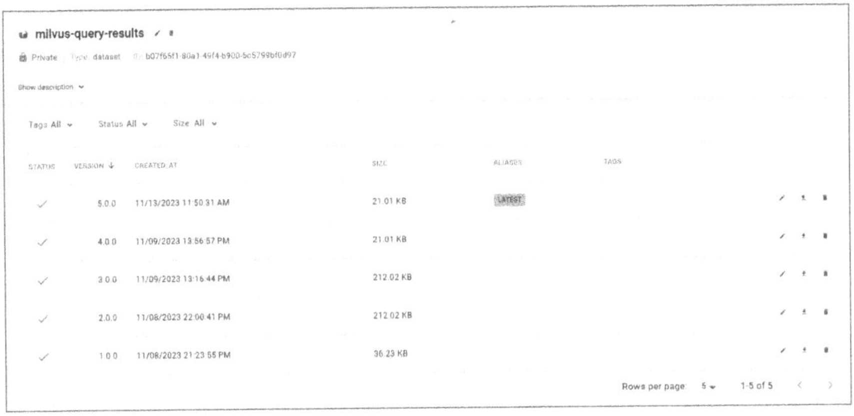

Figure 3.14 Data stored as an artifact

Figure 3.15 Data artifact as JSON

links to prepare data for analysis. Data engineering provides the tools to curate, cleanse, and transform raw data into a refined and optimized state. For data scientists, these principles are invaluable, as they guarantee a seamless analytical process without the hindrances of data silos, inconsistencies, or inefficiencies.

Knowing "Just Enough" Engineering

You don't need to be an expert in continuous integration/continuous delivery (CI/CD), but understanding data engineering principles is vital in data science.

data.json

File Type <> JSON   Size 21.01 KB   ⬇

 1 [
 2   {
 3   "author": "Kristen Kehrer",
 4   "part_id": 3,
 5   "max_part_id": 9,
 6   "text": "be used to connect to zilla's Cloud we're going to use t
 7   "id": "30634b24-7563-4f0d-bc54-d0d2b69c89da",
 8   "title": "Vector Similarity Search using Images with Zilliz"
 9   },
10   {
11   "author": "Kristen Kehrer",
12   "part_id": 4,
13   "max_part_id": 9,
14   "text": "now we need to set up our cloud so we will be first conn
15   "id": "691471dd-3b9a-4362-97b4-4bb9906e9d13",
16   "title": "Vector Similarity Search using Images with Zilliz"
17   },
18   {
19   "author": "Kristen Kehrer",
20   "part_id": 1,
21   "max_part_id": 9,
22   "text": "going to import images from Google Drive I'll make sure
23   "id": "69a98dae-53d1-4a9e-9441-7edfe404d830",
24   "title": "Vector Similarity Search using Images with Zilliz"

Figure 3.16 JSON for data artifact

In this chapter, we discussed how the data is the most crucial aspect in any machine learning project. This truly makes data engineering the backbone of any successful data science project. Data engineers ensure that data is accessible, clean, and organized, enabling data scientists to focus on the core of their work.

Several fundamental principles guide data engineering, such as data quality, transformation, and integration. These principles are essential for building reliable and scalable data pipelines:

- **Data quality:** Ensuring data accuracy and consistency is fundamental. Dirty or erroneous data can significantly impact the quality of machine learning models.

- **Data transformation:** Data must be transformed into the correct format, structure, and schema for analysis and modeling.

- **Data integration:** Data engineers integrate data from various sources, including databases, APIs, and streaming platforms.

- **Scalability:** The ability to scale data pipelines is crucial as data volumes grow. This requires knowledge of distributed computing frameworks like Apache Spark.

Data engineers widely adopt CI/CD practices to automate data pipeline building, testing, and deployment.

As a data scientist, you are vital in creating machine learning models that drive insights and predictions. Your primary responsibility is understanding data, developing models, and interpreting results. You don't need to be a CI/CD expert and are not responsible for managing the infrastructure. Still, you should do the following:

- Collaborate with data engineers to effectively communicate model requirements and data needs.

- Understand the deployment process for your models and work closely with DevOps or data engineering teams for seamless model deployment.

Having a working knowledge of the deployment process and understanding how this work fits into the broader data ecosystem will also give you a more informed perspective when scoping projects and determining what is feasible.

Data is your most important asset in a modeling project. Data engineering is often the unsung hero in making this data available. You then have the responsibility of ensuring that you monitor for bias, version your data for reproducibility, choose the appropriate tools for handling your data, and it's becoming more and more frequent to leverage ML algorithms that have already been trained on a dataset that is not your own. With your data ready, we'll discuss leveraging LLMs in Chapter 4.

Standing Up Your LLM

Much of what we've covered so far has been at a higher level of abstraction, with some illustrative projects included to demonstrate the key ideas you've learned. In this chapter, you'll start getting more hands-on with your models. Using large language models (LLMs) as a focal point, you'll learn the fundamentals of experiment management, model selection, and LLM inference, and you'll even get into fine-tuning. Throughout, you'll be building your own framework for performing inference with prompt engineering in mind.

As you approach each topic in this chapter, you'll be applying an MLOps-focused approach. For example, when you get into fine-tuning, you won't just be focused on improving your model's performance; you'll be exploring strategies for minimizing the computational cost of fine-tuning with minimal trade-offs around performance.

To start, you'll be selecting your LLM for the rest of the exercises in this chapter.

Selecting Your LLM

Model selection in both traditional machine learning and in the context of large language models is largely about your data. For example, using boosted trees on a smaller dataset will likely lead to overfitting, while attempting simple logistic regression on a high-dimensional dataset will almost certainly lead to poor performance. Selecting an

LLM is similar in the sense that particular qualities of your data will determine which models will or won't exhibit good performance on your task. The difference with LLMs is in the criteria we use to define "good performance."

In traditional machine learning, the modeling phase involves quite a bit of experimentation with your model architecture. The goal is to discover a particular architecture that finds the most signal in your dataset, given your particular constraints. Concepts like the *No Free Lunch* theorem have underscored the idea that there is a unique, optimal model for your particular task, and that by selecting one architecture over another, you can see enormous swings in performance. With large language models, the situation is somewhat different.

The No Free Lunch (NFL) theorem establishes that no optimization algorithm can universally perform better than others when averaged over all possible problems.[1] This theorem, introduced by mathematicians David Wolpert and William Macready in 1997, is grounded in the idea that an algorithm's performance is intrinsically tied to the specific nature of the problem it's applied to. Essentially, the theorem posits that an algorithm's superiority in solving one class of problems necessarily comes at the cost of its efficacy in others. For years, this line of thinking shaped the intuition of researchers in machine learning, leading to common sentiments like "Neural networks are the second best solution to every problem." In the 2010s, however, researchers began pushing the idea that while the NFL theorem was sound mathematically, it was being misapplied by many in the field and that generalist models were worth building.

---

[1]D.H. Wolpert, W.G. Macready, "No free lunch theorems for optimization", IEEE, April 1997, https://ieeexplore.ieee.org/document/585893

Large language models are generalists. As of this book's writing, OpenAI's GPT-4 scores highest on benchmarks for many different tasks. Even in highly specialized tasks like machine translation, GPT-4 is competitive with specialist systems, particularly for certain language pairings. This generalist trend has been apparent since the release of GPT-2 in 2018, and it shows no signs of slowing down in the near future. There are many situations where large foundation models like GPT-4 are not the top performers, and we'll dig into them later, but in general, the best model for your task is very likely the best model for most other tasks, at least in terms of raw performance.

Language Models Are Unsupervised Multitask Learners

The seminal "Language Models are Unsupervised Multitask Learners" paper from OpenAI Research introduced GPT-2 and marked a significant milestone in the evolution of language models.[2] In 2018, there were several landmark papers published that focused on the effectiveness of fine-tuning large pretrained language models for downstream tasks. These include the OpenAI paper that introduced GPT-2's predecessor, "Improving language understanding with unsupervised learning,"[3] as well as the paper that introduced the idea of universal language model

(continued)

---

[2]Alec Radford, Jeffrey Wu, Rewon Child, David Luan, Dario Amodei, and Ilya Sutskever, "Large language models are unsupervised multitask learners. 2019, arXiv, `https://cdn.openai.com/better-language-models/language_models_are_unsupervised_multitask_learners.pdf`
[3]Alec Radford, Karthik Narasimhan, Tim Salimans, and Ilya Sutskever, "Improving language understanding with unsupervised learning", June 2018, OpenAI, `https://openai.com/research/language-unsupervised`

(continued)

fine-tuning (ULMFiT), "Universal Language Model Fine-tuning for Text Classification,"[4] by Jeremy Howard and Sebastian Ruder. In 2019, just one year later, the OpenAI team released the language models paper, which showed that a large enough language model could be effective on multiple downstream tasks—without any fine-tuning.

The core of the paper details the architecture and training process of GPT-2. This large-scale transformer-based model has 1.5 billion parameters and was trained on a diverse range of Internet text. This training approach imbues GPT-2 with a broad understanding of language and context, enabling it to generate coherent and contextually relevant text across various topics and styles. Its ability to adapt to different tasks (such as text completion, translation, summarization, and even rudimentary conversation) without specific training sets it apart from earlier models. This multitasking capability paved the way for more flexible and comprehensive AI language systems like GPT-4.

Just because GPT-4 scores the highest on relevant benchmarks, however, does not make it the best model for your project. For example, if you work in an industry like healthcare, where you cannot share patients' medical data with third-party vendors, then you'll need to be more careful using GPT-4, as it can be accessed only via OpenAI's API. It's very likely, however, that with the right combination of fine-tuning and engineering, you can get the level of

---

[4] Jeremy Howard and Sebastian Ruder, "Universal Language Model Fine-tuning for Text Classification", January 2018, arXiv, `https://arxiv.org/abs/1801.06146`

performance you need out of models that you can host yourself, even if your model doesn't have the same power as GPT-4.

In other words, when you select an LLM, you cannot discern the "best" model via a simple accuracy metric. You have to evaluate the model against a complex criteria that includes factors such as privacy concerns, inference speed, available training data, and budget.

To perform this evaluation, you should break down each machine learning (ML)–dependent component in your project and ask a series of questions.

- What type of inference do I need to perform?
- How open-ended is this task?
- What are the privacy concerns for this data?
- How much will this model cost each time it runs inference, and how much inference are we expecting?

Let's do this with our YouTube retrieval project.

What Type of Inference Do I Need to Perform?

In the YouTube retrieval project, we have the following inference tasks:

- Embeddings generation for transcripts
- YouTube search query formation
- Question-answering over our documents

Thinking on a product level, our users will expect that when they input a question, they receive an answer relatively quickly. This means we will need to perform on-demand inference in real time. We won't be able to run scheduled batch inference offline; we'll need a highly available model that can perform inference whenever we need it.

Our choice is between using a third-party API, like GPT-4, and deploying our own LLM on cloud infrastructure powerful enough to perform real-time inference at scale. To decide between the two, we continue with our questions.

How Open-Ended Is This Task?

Some products, like a toxicity detector, have focused tasks that lend themselves well to fine-tuning. You can take a relatively small pre-trained language model, create a dataset of texts with "toxic" or "not toxic" labels, and fine-tune the model to classify the text with fantastic results. Other tasks are much more open-ended and require a highly flexible model.

Question-answering, as in the case of our YouTube retrieval project, falls on the open-ended side of the spectrum. Users can ask multifaceted questions involving mathematics or foreign languages, and our model needs to understand them. This requirement limits our model selection further. Hosted foundation models like GPT-4 are still an option, but if we elect to deploy our own model, we have to select a large enough model to support this complexity. GPT4All, accessible at gpt4all.io, is a fantastic resource that can assist you here. It provides a constantly updated listing of models suitable for local use.

What Are the Privacy Concerns for This Data?

This book is not going to wade too deeply into the topic of privacy regulation, as it is a constantly shifting landscape that varies across (and within) countries and depends on industry. However, regardless of where you are located, the best approach for evaluating your project's privacy concerns is to look at each component of your system, analyze the data required, and decide if any of the data is protected by regulation, and what permissions you have from the user concerning their data. For example, on an e-commerce site where a customer fills out their information to print on a business card, you may not have specifically asked the customer if you were able to leverage this data.

If you make the assumption that your application's UI warns users not to input any personally identifying information in their queries, then you do not have much to worry about here. Your documents are generated from publicly available YouTube videos, and you are not storing user information anywhere.

If your data did contain personal identifiable information (PII) that fell under regulatory protection, however, we'd likely be unable to use it with a third-party API without serious modifications, or without scrubbing the PII first. This could potentially be an option, depending on the use case.

How Much Will This Model Cost?

After answering the previous three questions about inference, open-endedness, and privacy, we are down to two options. We can do either of these:

- Deploy a model with billions of parameters onto cloud infrastructure provisioned with enough compute resources to perform real-time inference.

- Use a hosted foundation model like Anthropic's Claude or OpenAI's GPT-4.

To decide between the two, let's break down the costs.

Let's say the application has on average 1,000 daily active users. Those users, on average, perform 30 searches per day. The average search is roughly 50 tokens long, and the average response is roughly 250 tokens long.

67

As of the time of this book's writing, GPT-4 Turbo for the Azure OpenAI API costs $0.01 per 1,000 input tokens (a token is roughly 4 characters) and $0.03 per 1,000 output tokens. This means the average search would cost us $0.0105. The average user performing 30 searches per day costs us $0.315 per day. So, 1,000 daily active users at $0.315 per day brings us to $315, which over a 30-day month brings us to a total monthly price of $9,450.[5]

Now, let's look at the cost of deploying our own model to a cloud provider. To calculate this, we are just going to look at the price of the compute resources needed to host our model and perform inference. Note that in a real production environment, we would probably have additional services and resources deployed for things like autoscaling and failure management, which would incur additional costs.

The recommended instance type on AWS for hosting a 70 billion parameter model is the g5.48xlarge. This instance is provisioned with 192 GB of GPU memory and, if you're running it via AWS SageMaker, can cost as much as $20 per hour. That's $480 per day, or $14,440 per month. And remember, this is for one single instance. Because we have so many daily active users, we are almost certainly going to need multiple instances running at peak periods. If we average just two instances running per hour, our average monthly cost jumps to **$28,880**.

With all of this in mind, the obvious choice for our project is to use GPT-4. Now, let's get to actually experimenting with the model.

Experiment Management with LLMs

In this section, you'll learn how to run experiments on your language model in a structured, insightful way. This can be particularly

---

[5]OpenAI Pricing, `https://openai.com/pricing`

difficult for LLMs. With a traditional machine learning model, you can typically establish a numeric objective to optimize, like accuracy or precision. Because of how complex and open-ended LLM tasks often are, however, it's rarely as straightforward to measure their performance within your experiments. However, with the right tools and techniques, you can effectively experiment with your LLM to improve the overall performance of your system.

In machine learning, *experiment* is a somewhat nebulous term for "a single attempt at training a good model." Experiment management tools like Comet provide version control for all of your training data and outputs, including your dataset, hyperparameters, metrics, artifacts, models, and even training code. With this data preserved, you can investigate your models and reliably reproduce any experiment.

Prior to the release of experiment management tools like Comet, very few teams were performing statistical analysis and machine learning research in reproducible ways. Training runs were often tracked in spreadsheets, if at all. Code was run in notebooks, which were saved locally and rarely standardized. There were also very few systems for version controlling the actual training artifacts, like the model itself, and the systems that did exist were awkward and poorly adopted. Models were shared between data scientists via email, often with no recorded link between the dataset version, training code, or parameters used to train the model. This was not because data science teams were lazy or naïve; it was simply a hard problem. Version control systems like Git don't work well for machine learning, where datasets and models can be massive, unreadable files. Notebooks themselves are difficult to version control in a meaningful way due to the way they operate under the hood. And tracking the lineage of a dataset, the parameters of each training run, the code used, the systems training was conducted on, and all the other variables involved in training represents an incredibly complex attribution challenge that goes beyond the traditional version control systems from software engineering. It wasn't until the mid-to-late 2010s that vendors started to emerge with real solutions to this complex problem.

In this next exercise, you'll use experiment management in the context of inference. This is somewhat nontraditional, but because you are working with LLMs, the approach is warranted. With LLMs, you are commonly constructing complex pipelines for inference, along with nuanced prompting strategies. Building such an inference pipeline requires an iterative approach, one that generates reproducible results. In that light, experiment management is a natural solution.

To begin, you'll set up your model for inference. The first thing you'll need is to create a few functions for interacting with your API and generating your prompts. You could use a tool like LangChain for this, but in this project, you'll implement your functions from scratch to make things as transparent as possible.

First, create some dictionaries to hold your prompt templates—these are essentially template strings you use to prompt your model—and then create a function to generate prompts on the fly.

```
##Define a dictionary containing prompts for different
types of queries
PROMPTS = {
    "math": """Please answer the following mathematics
question. If you don't know the answer, respond
"I don't know." \n Question: {question}"""
}
```

```
##Define system prompts associated with different
prompt types
SYSTEM_PROMPTS = {
    "math": "You are a helpful assistant who solves
math problems for users."
}
##Function to generate message for the AI chat system
def generate_messages(prompt_id, system_prompt_id =
None, prompt_variables = {}):
    user_prompt = PROMPTS[prompt_id].format
(**prompt_variables)
    system_prompt = SYSTEM_PROMPTS[prompt_id] if
system_prompt_id is None else
SYSTEM_PROMPTS[system_prompt_id]
##Return system and user messages in a list format
    return [
        {"role": "system", "content": system_prompt},
        {"role": "user", "content": user_prompt}
    ]
```

Next, write a function to interact with the GPT-4 API.

```
from openai import OpenAI
import comet_llm
openai_client = OpenAI(api_key="YOUR-API-KEY")
comet_llm.init(api_key="YOUR-COMET-API-KEY")
def get_completion(
    prompt_id,
    system_prompt_id = None,
    prompt_variables = None,
    model="gpt-4-1106-preview",
    temperature=0,
    max_tokens=2000,
):
```

```
##Generate messages using the provided inputs
    messages = generate_messages(prompt_id, system_
prompt_id, prompt_variables)
##Call an OpenAI function to get completions based on
the generated messages.
    response = openai_client.chat.completions.create(
        model=model,
        messages=messages,
        temperature=temperature,
        max_tokens=max_tokens,
    )
##Log the prompt, completion, and related metadata
    comet_llm.log_prompt(
        prompt=messages[1]['content'],
        prompt_template=PROMPTS[prompt_id],
        prompt_template_variables=prompt_variables,
        metadata= {
            "usage.prompt_tokens": response.usage.
prompt_tokens,
            "usage.completion_tokens": response.usage.
completion_tokens,
            "usage.total_tokens": response.usage.
total_tokens,
            "system_fingerprint" response.system_
fingerprint
        },
        output=response.choices[0].message.content,
    )
##return the response
    return response.choices[0].message.content
```

You can tweak any of the parameters, including the model, as you like. For example, you might use a cheaper model initially in your setup phase as you iron out errors and minor bugs. You'll notice that you used Comet LLM to log your prompt and response. Take a look at how that actually works by running a test inference now. Try running the following code:

```
question = {
    "question": "What three-digit palindromes are also
perfect squares?"
}
get_completion(prompt_id="math",
prompt_variables=question)
```

If you're using GPT-4, you should see output like this:

```
A palindrome is a number that reads the same forwards
and backwards. A three-digit palindrome must be of
the form "ABA", where A and B are digits, with A not
being 0 (since we want a three-digit number).... The
three-digit palindromes that are also perfect squares
are 121, 484, and 676.
```

When you navigate to your experiment dashboard in Comet, you will see the information you logged, as shown in Figure 4.1.

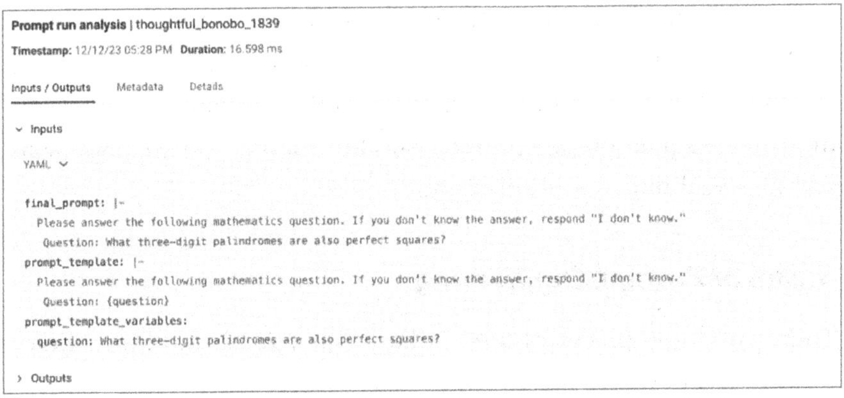

Figure 4.1   Experiment dashboard

With this little bit of code, you now have a system in place that will automatically log all of your interactions with your LLM, allowing you to reproduce specific inferences and debug the performance of different prompts and parameters.

Now, you can start experimenting.

LLM Inference

With a traditional machine learning model, improving model performance typically comes down to modifying the model itself, either by tweaking hyperparameters or by subjecting it to additional training. With large language models, another way to improve model performance is by being thoughtful and strategic about your prompts.

While you can, of course, fine-tune an LLM to change its behavior, it is often the case that the capability you're looking for is already in the model weights—you just have to access it. The key to doing this is to prompt the model correctly. Unfortunately, much of the writing around prompting LLMs is haphazard, composed mostly as a compendium of random hacks. This section devoted to teaching you not just a list of techniques for prompting your model but a methodical system for crafting the empirically best prompt possible.

You should also note that this section avoids some of the terminology you may see in contemporary discourse around prompting LLMs, particularly as it applies to specific prompting techniques and strategies. The focus in this section is on the fundamental ideas that these techniques employ, which should enable you to understand any new technique you encounter.

Basics of Prompt Engineering

There are a few pieces of terminology that you should know before diving too deep into the world of LLM inference.

The chain of input tokens an LLM uses to predict the most likely output token is referred to as *context*. The maximum length of contextual input the model can accept defines the boundary of the model's *context window*, which "slides" across the text as the model outputs new tokens. A *prompt* is input you provide to initiate inference. A *prompt template* typically refers to the skeleton of a prompt that is dynamically loaded with your data, for example:

```
Instruction_template = ```
INSTRUCTION:
Write a Python script that satisfies the following
request: {{YOUR REQUEST}}
ANSWER:
```
```

Different models will have their own prompt template based on the way they were built. The prompt template, in this case, is analogous to the preprocessing of data before inference in traditional machine learning.

When you hear prompting discussed in the world of generative AI, however, you will typically hear it discussed in the context of *prompt engineering*. Prompt engineering refers to the work of crafting a prompt to elicit the particular response you are looking for. For example, to force the model to respond with a longer, more reasoned answer, you might append "Let's think step-by-step." to the end of your prompt. Many are skeptical of prompt engineering as a real discipline, viewing it as largely unscientific tinkering. We're going to challenge that assumption in this book by viewing prompt engineering as a complex optimization problem, one that will require meaningful engineering effort to solve efficiently.

When an LLM outputs a given word, it is simply sampling from a probability distribution of likely next tokens. For example, if you
```

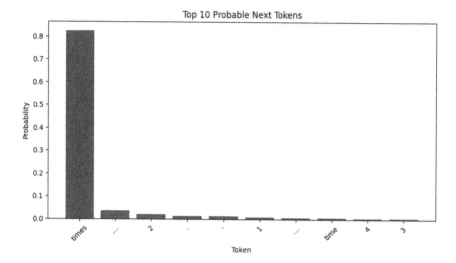

Figure 4.2 Top 10 probable next tokens

were to input the prompt "It was the best of times, it was the worst of" to an LLM, your distribution of next tokens might look like the chart in Figure 4.2.

The chart in Figure 4.2 is taken from a 7 billion parameter Mistral model.

When you alter the prompt, you alter the sequence of words leading up to this next token and thereby condition the distribution of likely next tokens. This allows you to impact the conditional probabilities of your model without gradient updates. If you can dynamically select the right prompt, this means you have effectively increased the expressivity of your model without any drop in performance across tasks.

For the rest of this book, we will think of prompting as a way to update the token distribution *without updating the underlying weights*. It provides the *benefits* of fine-tuning a model for a downstream task without the *cost* of fine-tuning.

Naturally, there are trade-offs associated with prompt engineering. Adding extra tokens to your prompt increases the number of computations needed to predict the next token, thereby increasing the compute footprint of your inference. Some of the techniques described in subsequent sections take this to an extreme, featuring recursive calls to LLMs to both generate and evaluate output before arriving at a final response. Obviously, all of this extra computation comes at a price.

In the upcoming sections, you will be implementing several different prompting techniques and evaluating their performance. There are many frameworks that make it simple to experiment with prompt engineering, and in the appendix, you will find recommendations for some fantastic frameworks. For now, however, you are going to be building your own prompting micro-framework. The goal here is not to produce a production-ready framework but rather to give you a bottoms-up understanding of what goes into building an inference pipeline.

In-Context Learning

Most prompting techniques generally fall under the umbrella of in-context learning. With in-context learning, you give the model additional information to assist with inference, but instead of training the model on this additional information, you pass it in via your prompt (the context window).

As an example, imagine you wanted your model to write a Python script that will organize your notes. However, you write your notes using a text editor that stores data in a peculiar way, one that requires you to use the editor's API to export your data. Your model may have not been trained on any examples featuring this proprietary API, so it will not do a good job of generating your script on its own. However, if you pass the API's documentation—or even just some examples of other scripts made with the API—into the context window, your model may be able to write a usable Python script.

You can also understand in-context learning using the same visualization technique from the previous section (the code is available at this book's GitHub). Using the same model that generated the distribution for "It was the best of times, it was the worst of," you can pass in a math problem like "6^3 - 17 = " and visualize a distribution as shown in Figure 4.3.

6^3 - 17 is actually equal to 199, but the model is unsure. It is very close to selecting the correct first digit, but it still leans toward 2 over 1, which will, of course, send it down the incorrect sequence.

If, however, you give the model a related problem in its context window, things change. Passing in "6^3 - 25 = 191" before "6^3 - 17 =" yields the distribution shown in Figure 4.4.

With 1, the correct next token is by far the most likely selection.

In this section, you'll implement the first parts of your prompt engineering framework. In your framework, you are going to conceptualize the entire inference process as a pipeline, with each

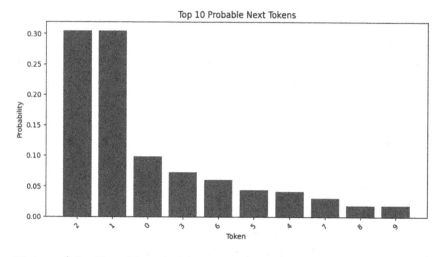

Figure 4.3 Top 10 probable next tokens based on math problem

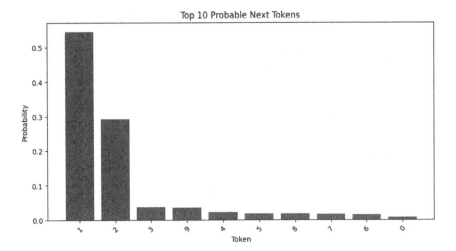

Figure 4.4 Top 10 probable next tokens based on context

individual operation encapsulated in a node. This will make it much easier to experiment with your prompts in a reproducible way.

First, you'll need some basic utilities, including a method for generating predictions as well as an initialized OpenAI client. The following code implements this for you:

```
import os
from openai import OpenAI
from abc import ABC, abstractmethod
client = OpenAI(api_key="YOUR-API-KEY")
def get_completion(
    prompt,
    model="gpt-3.5-turbo-instruct",
    temperature=0,
    max_tokens=2000,
    return_full=False,
    **kwargs
):
```

Standing Up Your LLM

```
response = client.completions.create(
    model=model,
    prompt=prompt,
    temperature=temperature,
    max_tokens=max_tokens,
    **kwargs
)
if return_full:
    return response
return response.choices[0].text
```

The get_completions() method uses OpenAI's comple-tion API to run inference on your prompt and then returns the top prediction.

Next, establish an abstract class for your Pipeline and Node classes.

```
class Node(ABC):
    @abstractmethod
    def forward(self):
        pass
class Pipeline(ABC):
    @abstractmethod
    def run(self):
        pass
```

These aren't much to look at right now, but that's the idea. You will build this mini-framework in small, discrete steps to better understand what is actually happening under the hood in some of the more popular LLM frameworks. Note that the Node class has a forward() method, similar to modules in PyTorch. This should give you some notion of how we are going to stack nodes inside a pipeline.

Finally, you'll implement a `PromptNode`, which simply applies a prompt template to a prompt and queries your model via a `generate()` callback.

```
class PromptNode(Node):
    def __init__(self, prompt_template,
generate=get_completion):
        self.prompt_template = prompt_template
        self.generate = generate
        self.prompt = None
    def forward(self, **kwargs):
        self.prompt = self.prompt_template.format
(**kwargs)
        return self.generate(self.prompt)
```

Notice that the `PromptNode` class sets the `generate()` function as your `get_completion()` function by default, but you can define any custom inference function you'd like for your node to use.

Now, you can experiment with some simple in-context learning. A classic example, inspired by the original GPT-4 paper, is a translation task. Try translating a complex sentence into a less common language. For example, try translating "It was the best of times, it was the worst of times." into Tigrinya, an Afro-Asiatic language.

To start, make a simple template for translating text into Tigrinya.

```
translate_tigrinya = """Translate the following
into Tigrinya:
{prompt} => """
```

Now, create a pipeline class for the task.

```
class TigrinyaTranslatePipeline(Pipeline):
    def __init__(self):
        self.p1 = PromptNode(prompt_template=
translate_tigrinya)
    def run(self, **kwargs):
        return self.p1.forward(**kwargs)
```

Run the pipeline.

```
no_icl = TigrinyaTranslatePipeline()
no_icl.run(prompt="It was the best of times, it was
the worst of times.")
```

Testing the previous code with GPT-3.5, you will probably see a response that looks something like this repeating for many lines:

` \nኣብ ኣብዚ. ኣብ ኣብዚ. ኣብ ኣብዚ. ኣብ ኣብዚ. ኣብ ኣብዚ. ኣብ ኣብዚ. ኣብ ኣብዚ. ኣብ ኣብዚ. ኣብ ኣብዚ. ኣብ ኣብዚ. ኣብ ኣብዚ. ኣብ ኣብዚ. ኣብ ኣብዚ. ኣብ ኣብዚ. ኣብ ኣብዚ. ኣብ ኣብዚ. ኣብ ኣብዚ. .

Putting a snippet of the response into Google Translate returns "At this in here in here in here. . ." It seems the model is confused by the sentence structure, getting stuck in an endless loop.

Perhaps giving the model an example of a similar sentence in Tigrinya will help. Try creating a new template with a few example sentences and updating the pipeline to use it.

```
translate_tigrinya_icl = """Translate the following
into Tigrinya:
It was the age of wisdom, it was the age of
foolishness. => ዘመነ ጥበብ እዩ ነይሩ፡ ዘመነ ዕሽነት እዩ ነይሩ።
Translate the following into Tigrinya:
To be, or not to be, that is the question. => ምኽኒን
ዘይምህላውን፡ እቲ ሕቶ ንሱ እዩ።
```

```
Translate the following into Tigrinya:
What happiness was ours that day, what joy, what rest,
what hope, what gratitude, what bliss! => ኣብታ መዓልቲ
እቲኣ ከመይ ዝበለ ሓጎስ እዩ ነይሩ፣ ከመይ ዝበለ ሓጎስ፣ ከመይ ዝበለ ዕረፍቲ፣ ከመይ
ዝበለ ተስፋ፣ ከመይ ዝበለ ምስጋና፣ ከመይ ዝበለ ዕግበት !
Translate the following into Tigrinya:
{prompt} => """
class TigrinyaTranslatePipeline(Pipeline):
    def __init__(self, icl=None):
        if icl == 'icl' :
            self.p1 =
PromptNode(prompt_template=translate_tigrinya_icl)
        else:
            self.p1 =
PromptNode(prompt_template=translate_tigrinya)
    def run(self, **kwargs):
        return self.p1.forward(**kwargs)
icl = TigrinyaTranslatePipeline(icl="icl")
icl.run(prompt="It was the best of times, it was the
worst of times.")
```

Beyond the new template, the only real change to the code is
the introduction of the icl (in-context learning) argument for the
TigrinyaTranslatePipeline class. Running this pipeline,
you'll see results that look like this:

ዘመነ ኣብ ዝበለ ጊዜ እዩ ነይሩ፣ ዘመነ ኣብ ዝበለ ጊዜ እዩ ነይሩ።

This, according to Google Translate, works out to "It was at the
right time, it was at the right time." That's not quite a correct translation, but it's much closer to the goal than the first attempt.

Experiment further by expanding the template to include even
more translations. For the sake of brevity, the following is truncated.

Standing Up Your LLM

```
translate_tigrinya_icl_ext = """Translate the
following into Tigrinya:
Shall I compare thee to a summer's day? => ምስ መዓልቲ
ሓጋይዶ ክወዳድረካ እየ፧
Translate the following into Tigrinya:
Four score and seven years ago our fathers brought
forth on this continent, a new nation, conceived in
Liberty, and dedicated to the proposition that all men
are created equal. => ቅድሚ 87 ዓመት ኣቦታትና ኣብዛ ኣህጉር እዚኣ፡ ኣብ
ሓርነት ዝተሓስበ፡ ኩሎም ደቂ ሰባት ማዕረ ተፈጢሮም ንዝብል ሓሳብ ዝተወፈየ ሓድሽ
ህዝቢ ኣምጺኦም እዮም።
. . .
Translate the following into Tigrinya:
{prompt} => """
class TigrinyaTranslatePipeline(Pipeline):
    def __init__(self, icl=None):
        if icl == 'icl' :
            self.p1 =
PromptNode(prompt_template=translate_tigrinya_icl)
        elif icl == 'icl_ext':
            self.p1 =
PromptNode(prompt_template=translate_tigrinya_icl_ext)
        else:
            self.p1 =
PromptNode(prompt_template=translate_tigrinya)
    def run(self, **kwargs):
        return self.p1.forward(**kwargs)
icl_ext = TigrinyaTranslatePipeline(icl="icl_ext")
icl_ext.run(prompt="It was the best of times, it was
the worst of times.")
```

The previous should return something like this:

ዘመነ ንፍረት ኡየ ነይሩ፥ ዘመነ ሕማቅ ኡየ ነይሩ።

This translates to the mostly correct "It was a fruitful era, it was a bad era."

In this example, you've seen the essential value and tension of in-context learning. The more relevant context you fit in the window, the more accurate your model will perform. At the same time, the more context you include, the more expensive your inference becomes. Effective in-context learning is about ensuring you include the most relevant and minimal context for each inference. Later sections explore this dynamic process in more detail.

Intermediary Computation

One of the fundamental concepts in LLM inference is something called *intermediary computation*. When you use intermediary computation, you guide your model's inference such that it generates output in a longer, typically more structured way. Intuitively, this is similar to the way humans apply variable amounts of computation to reasoning tasks (though of course, it is always dangerous to anthropomorphize models too heavily). If you are asked to calculate 2 + 2, you know the answer immediately. If you are given a complex calculating with exponents and several different operations, you will likely answer more slowly, addressing each subproblem individually before completing the entire equation.

Intermediary computation crops up all over the field of prompt engineering. For example, recent papers have found that when asking a model to evaluate a snippet of code, instructing the model to write out the stack trace of the program at each line using a "scratchpad" significantly increases its accuracy. Similarly, many of the most popular LLM frameworks today have out-of-the-box prompting techniques that increase intermediary computation for models.

> ### Chain-of-Thought Prompting Elicits Reasoning in Large Language Models
>
> In 2023, a team at Google Brain released a paper titled "Chain-of-Thought Prompting Elicits Reasoning in Large Language Models,"[6] which introduced a new technique for prompting models. The core insight was that by forcing a model to answer a question step-by-step (or at least, providing it with step-by-step reasoning in its context window), you could elicit much better responses.
>
> These techniques were not without precedent—the idea of "prompt engineering" had been around for years at this point. But the results themselves were staggering. On complex questions, such as arithmetic problems, commonsense reasoning, or even science-based questions, the researchers were able to produce performance from a 540 billion parameter model that rivaled that of some of the largest available LLMs.
>
> This publication kicked off a wave of new research into related techniques, including the so-called "Tree of Thought,"[7] which combines ideas from search algorithms to chain-of-thought approaches. Today, almost all major LLM frameworks incorporate chain-of-thought techniques in one way or another.

---

[6]Jason Wei, Xuezhi Wang, Dale Schuurmans, Maarten Bosma, Brian Ichter, Fei Xia, Ed Chi, Quoc Le, and Denny Zhou, "Chain-of-Thought Prompting Elicits Reasoning in Large Language Models", January 2022, arXiv, https://arxiv.org/abs/2201.11903

[7]Shunyu Yao, Dian Yu, Jeffrey Zhao, Izhak Shafran, Thomas L. Griffiths, Yuan Cao, and Karthik Narasimhan, "Tree of Thoughts: Deliberate Problem Solving with Large Language Models", May 2023, arXiv, https://arxiv.org/abs/2305.10601

You may have heard of a family of techniques called *chain-of-thought prompting*. These are, essentially, a form of in-context learning designed to leverage intermediary computation to guide inference. The first published chain-of-thought examples looked a lot like the translation project you implemented in the previous section. The model was fed a series of example tasks that mimicked the prompt, before being given the actual prompt. Since then, many related techniques have been proposed, oftentimes focused on techniques for dynamically composing the most effective "chain" of inputs for a given task.

Interestingly however, one of the most effective chain-of-thought techniques doesn't require you to input any extra examples into the context window at all. In 2022, a team of researchers from the University of Tokyo and Google Research introduced what they call "zero-shot-CoT" prompting in their paper "Large Language Models are Zero-Shot Reasoners."[8] It turns out, simply adding "Let's think step-by-step" to the beginning of the model's response will guide it toward longer, step-by-step reasoning, which increases the intermediary computation and ultimately the accuracy of the inference.

You can experiment with this easily. The following code implements a simple chain-of-thought prompt for solving equations and compares it to an identical prompt without a chain-of-thought prefix:

```
math_template = """INSTRUCTION:
Solve the following equation: {prompt}
```

[8]Takeshi Kojima, Shixiang Shane Gu, Machel Reid, Yutaka Matsuo, and Yusuke Iwasawa, "Large Language Models are Zero-Shot Reasoners", May 2022, arXiv, https://arxiv.org/abs/2205.11916

RESPONSE:

```
"""
class EquationPipeline(Pipeline):
    def __init__(self, with_zero_shot_cot=False):
        if with_zero_shot_cot is True:
            self.p1 = PromptNode(prompt_template=math_
template + "Let's think step by step. ")
        else:
            self.p1 =
PromptNode(prompt_template=math_template)
    def run(self, **kwargs):
        return self.p1.forward(**kwargs)
equation = "6^8 * 2 / 3 + 7 - 1 ="
raw_pipeline = EquationPipeline()
cot_pipeline =
EquationPipeline(with_zero_shot_cot=True)
print("Without Chain of Thought Prompting")
print(raw_pipeline.run(prompt=equation))
print("With Chain of Thought Prompting")
print(cot_pipeline.run(prompt=equation))
```

Running this code should output something like this:

```
Without Chain of Thought Prompting
6^8 * 2 / 3 + 7 - 1 = 2,176,782,337.333333 + 7 - 1 =
2,176,782,343.333333
With Chain of Thought Prompting
Step 1: Simplify the exponent
6^8 = 1679616
Step 2: Multiply 1679616 by 2
1679616 * 2 = 3359232
Step 3: Divide by 3
3359232 / 3 = 1119744
Step 4: Add 7
```

```
1119744 + 7 = 1119751
Step 5: Subtract 1
1119751 - 1 = 1119750
Therefore, the solution to the equation is 1119750.
```

As you can see, simply adding "Let's think step-by-step" to the model's response guides it toward a cleaner, deliberate path of reasoning, which ultimately results in the correct answer.

There are many prompting techniques built around this idea of intermediary computation, and you'll implement some of the more complex ones shortly.

Augmented Generation

Building on the idea of in-context learning, there are many popular inference techniques for LLMs that rely on additional processes, oftentimes unrelated to the LLM itself, to dynamically generate context. You'll often hear these techniques brought up in the context of agents—something covered in the next section—and referred to as *tools*.

In previous chapters, you've seen some basic examples of retrieval augmented generation (RAG), in which your inference pipeline involves a process for querying outside information at inference time. This is particularly useful for tasks involving information that is more recent than your model's latest training run (commonly referred to as the model's *knowledge cutoff*).

In this next example, you'll implement a simple RAG pipeline that uses YouTube transcripts to answer questions.

The first thing you'll need to implement is a retriever node, which fetches and transforms your data. You're going to use two popular open-source libraries fetching your YouTube videos and their transcripts. In addition, you will make multiple calls to the LLM, one to produce a good YouTube search query and another to summarize the first section of each video. You will be parsing only a short section from each video, due to limits in the context window of your models. In later sections, you will learn how to more dynamically select the information you include in your context window.

Listing 4.1 shows the code for your YouTubeRetriever.

Listing 4.1 YouTubeReceiver

```
from youtube_transcript_api import
YouTubeTranscriptApi
from youtube_search import YoutubeSearch

class YouTubeRetriever(Node):
    def __init__(self, generate=get_completion):
        self.generate = generate
    def _fetch_transcripts(self, query):
        results = YoutubeSearch(query, max_results=
10).to_dict()
        return [ f"['url_suffix'].split('&')[0]}" for
x in results ]
    def _parse_transcript(self, transcript, video_id):
        full_text = "
        arr = transcript[0][video_id]
        for obj in arr:
            full_text += f"{obj['text']} "
        return full_text
    def _summarize_transcript(self, transcript):
        summary = self.generate(prompt=f"""INSTRUCTION:
\nBelow is a transcript generated from a YouTube
video. Condense and summarize it.\n\n"{transcript}"\
nRESPONSE:\n""").strip()
```

```
        return summary

    def forward(self, question):
        context = ""
        # Generate search term + strip leading/
trailing newlines and quotation marks
        youtube_query = self.generate(prompt=youtube_
query_template.format(prompt=question)).strip().
strip("\"")
        results = YoutubeSearch(youtube_query, max_
results=10).to_dict()
        for x in results:
            video_id = x['id']
            transcript = ""
            try:
                transcript = YouTubeTranscriptApi.get_
transcripts(video_ids=[video_id])
                transcript = self._parse_transcript
(transcript, video_id)
                if len(transcript) > 2000:
                    transcript = transcript[0:2000]
                transcript = self._summarize_
transcript(transcript)
            except TranscriptsDisabled:
                print(f"Transcripts disabled for
{x['title']}")
                pass
            snippet = f"{x['title']} by {x['channel']}
\n\n{transcript}\n\n"
            context += snippet
        return context
```

From here, you can add your retriever node to a pipeline and perform inference:

```
class QAWithYoutubePipeline(Pipeline):
    def __init__(self):
        self.context = ""
        self.retriever = YouTubeRetriever()
        self.qa = PromptNode(prompt_template=
"#INSTRUCTION:\nBelow, you have summaries from several
YouTube videos:\n\n{context}Use the above summaries to
answer this question: {question}\n#RESPONSE:\n")
    def run(self, question):
        self.context = self.retriever.forward
(question=question)
        return self.qa.forward(context=self.context,
question=question)
```

For comparison, try asking the model about a subject that is beyond its knowledge cutoff with and without the retriever node. For example, if you ask GPT-3.5 about the Mixtral 8x-7b model that was released in late 2023, you will get a response like this:

```
get_completion(prompt="What is Mixtral 8x-7b?")
> 'Mixtral 8x-7b is not a known mathematical
expression or equation. It is possible that it is a
product or brand name, but without further context or
information, it is not possible to determine
its meaning.'
```

However, if you use the pipeline you just created, you'll see something different.

```
pipe = QAWithYoutubePipeline()
pipe.run("What is Mixtral 8x-7b?")
> "Mixtral 8x-7b is a new language model developed by
Mistral AI that combines eight of their previous
models into one. It uses a mixture of experts
architecture, with multiple networks or experts and a
gating layer that decides which expert to allocate an
input to. It has gained attention in the AI world and
has been shown to outperform a 70 billion parameter
model while being four times faster. It is available
in three models: tiny, small, and medium, with the
medium model being the most expensive. It has been
compared to GPT-4 and has been found to be competitive
and possibly cheaper in terms of pricing. It is also
available through Mistral's development platform and
API in beta preview."
```

If you inspect the context, you'll see something like the following (note this is truncated to just one summary, whereas in reality, you will have several in your context window):

```
pipe.context
> "Mistral 8x7B Part 1- So What is a Mixture of
Experts Model? by Sam Witteveen
Mistral recently released a new model, the Mixture of
Experts, which combines eight of their previous models
into one. This concept is not new in the field of AI,
but with the advancement of technology, it is now
possible to implement it effectively. However, running
this model locally would require a significant amount
of computing power. The Mixture of Experts works by
having multiple networks, or experts, and a gating
layer that decides which expert to allocate an input
```

to. This concept is also related to GPT 4 and there are already similar models available."

In Chapter 5, you'll look at more complex, real-world RAG pipelines involving vector databases and dynamic context composition, but the goal here is to understand the basic idea. It is important to note that augmented generation is not restricted to document retrieval. It can include any additional source of input, including function calls to other models, third-party APIs, and so forth.

Agentic Techniques

The term *agent* is a somewhat controversial and poorly defined term in the world of large language models. It comes from the world of reinforcement learning, in which agents make decisions relative to a decision-making policy within an environment. The term *agent* is loosely used in the context of LLMs to refer to techniques in which a model is prompted to perform a series of inferences in a dynamic, sometimes recursive way. Often, an agent will use "tools" like the augmented generation techniques you implemented previously.

As a simple example, consider implementing a customer support agent. Imagine you've written three functions, or tools, for your agent to use:

- `translate_to_en()`: Uses the Google Translate API to translate non-English text

- `search_support_docs()`: Searches your internal documentation for relevant documents

- `search_web()`: Uses the Bing API to pull search results for a query

You might then prompt your customer support agent to use the appropriate tool when responding to the user's request. You might even give the agent a specific decision-making process, instructing it to translate any non-English text first, then use that output to query your support docs, and finally search the Web as a last resort if you cannot find any relevant documentation.

ReAct: Synergizing Reasoning and Acting in Language Models[9]

Historically, the development of language models has been primarily focused on enhancing their ability to understand and generate human-like text, while other fields focused on training models for decision-making. The "ReAct: Synergizing Reasoning and Acting in Language Models" paper marked a shift in this approach, introducing the idea that large language models were not just good at decision-making but that by combining reasoning and action-focused tasks, you could actually reveal overall enhanced capabilities in language models.

The core contribution of the paper lies in its novel approach to integrate reasoning and act within the structure of language models. The authors give the model normal question-and-answer tasks, but the model goes through a recursive process of analyzing the task, using appropriate tools (in this case, custom

(continued)

---

[9]Shunyu Yao, Jeffrey Zhao, Dian Yu, Nan Du, Izhak Shafran, Karthik Narasimhan, and Yuan Cao, "ReAct: Synergizing Reasoning and Acting in Language Models", October 2022, arXiv, https://arxiv.org/abs/2210.03629

95

(continued)

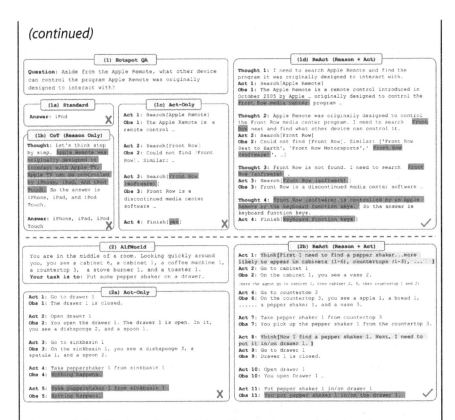

Figure 4.5 "ReAct: Synergizing Reasoning and Acting in Language Models" illustration

functions programmed for it), and building a useful context before answering. Figure 4.5 is taken directly from the paper.

In the realm of prompt engineering, the implications of this paper are profound. It provides a new paradigm where prompts are no longer just about eliciting responses but are also about guiding the model to perform specific actions. This elevates the role of prompt engineering from crafting text for optimal text generation to designing prompts that effectively integrate reasoning and action.

You are going to create an incredibly simple agent in this example. Your agent will have access to the YouTube search pipeline you built in Listing 4.1, as well as an additional translation function, defined here:

```
from deep_translator import GoogleTranslator
def translate(text, lang):
    translation = GoogleTranslator(source='auto',
target=lang).translate(text, dest=lang)
    return translation
```

Your agent will be given a question to answer, and it will use the tools available to do so. To implement this, first you need to set up a node for your translation function.

```
class TranslateNode(Node):
    def __init__(self, generate_fn=get_completion):
        self.preprocessing = """#INSTRUCTION:\n\nFrom
the following text, extract the sequences that are
written in {lang}:\n\n"{text}"\n\n#RESPONSE:\n\n"""
        self.generate = generate_fn

    def forward(self, text, generate=get_completion):
        extracted_text = self.generate(self.
preprocessing.format(text=text, lang="en"))[1:-1]
# Remove wrapping quotation marks
        translated_text = translate(extracted_text,
"en")
        translated = text.replace(extracted_text,
translated_text)
        return translated
```

Next, you'll need to set up your templates.

```python
tools = {
    "translate": {
        "description": """translate(text, lang) ->
This function takes input text and translates it to
the "lang" language.""",
        "node": TranslateNode,
        "transform_q": True
    },
    "YouTubeResearch": {
        "description": """YouTubeResearch(question) ->
This function takes a question and uses YouTube to
generate research around the question topic. Before
using, you should translate any non-English questions
into English.""",
        "node": QAWithYoutubePipeline,
        "transform_q": False
    }
}
tools_context = """#INSTRUCTION: You are a helpful
assistant who is capable of running Python functions.
You answer questions, but you only respond in English.
You have the following functions available to
you as tools:
{tools}
Do you need a tool to answer the following question
in English?
"{question}"
Respond "yes" or "no"
#RESPONSE: """
which_tool = """#INSTRUCTION: Which tool do you need?
You can respond with {tool_names}
#RESPONSE: """
```

```
final_q = """#INSTRUCTION: Write a response that
accurately answers the following question in English:
"{question}"
#RESPONSE: """
```

As you can see, you have a series of templates, as well as a dictionary titled tools, which you will use later in your agent.

Now, you can actually define your agent class, as shown in Listing 4.2. Note that an agent is just a pipeline under the hood.

Listing 4.2 Defining the Agent Class

```
import copy
class QAAgent(Pipeline):
    def __init__(self, tools=tools,
generate_fn=get_completion):
        self.generate = generate_fn
        self.translate = TranslateNode()
        self.youtube = QAWithYoutubePipeline()
        self.context = ""
        self.tools = tools
        self.available_tools = copy.deepcopy(tools)
    def _intermediary_step(self):
        formatted_tools = ""
        need_tool = ""
        next_tool = ""
        tool_context = ""
        selected_tool = None
        self.context = "" # Clear context
        for tool in self.available_tools.keys():
            formatted_tools += self.available_tools
[tool]['description']
            formatted_tools += "\n"
        need_tool_input = tools_context.format
(tools=formatted_tools, question=self.question)
```

```python
        need_tool = self.generate(need_tool_input)
        self.context += need_tool_input  + "\n\n" +
need_tool + "\n\n"

        if "yes" in need_tool.lower():
            tool_names = " or ".join(self.available_
tools.keys())
            next_tool = self.generate(self.context +
which_tool.format(tool_names=tool_names))
            self.context += which_tool.format(tool_
names = tool_names) + "\n\n" + next_tool + "\n\n"
            for name in self.available_tools.keys():
                if name in next_tool:
                    selected_tool = name
                    break

        return selected_tool

    def run(self, question):
        self.question = question
        selected_tool = self._intermediary_step()

        while len(self.available_tools.keys()) > 0:
            selected_tool = self._intermediary_step()

            if selected_tool == None:
                break

            next = self.tools[selected_tool]['node']()

            if hasattr(next, 'forward'):
                output = next.forward(self.question)
            else:
```

```
            output = next.run(self.question)
            if self.tools[selected_tool]['transform_
q'] == True:
                self.question = output
            self.context += output

            del self.available_tools[selected_tool]
        self.context += final_q.format(question=
self.question)
        answer = self.generate(self.context)
        self.available_tools = copy.deepcopy
(self.tools)
        return answer
```

If the code in Listing 4.2 is confusing, spend some time with it. Context management is key when working with agentic techniques. In a real-world setting, you will likely be using a much more complex memory structure than what you have here, but for demonstration purposes, this is all you need.

Now, if you run your agent, you will see that it is capable of fielding questions in different languages about topics it is unfamiliar with. For example, if you ask it "What is this LLMLingua project everyone is talking about?" in Spanish, you will get a response like this:

```
agent = QAAgent()
agent.run("¿Qué; es este proyecto LLMLingua del que
todo el mundo habla?")
> LLMLingua is a project developed by Microsoft that
aims to improve the efficiency and cost-effectiveness
of large language models used in AI. It utilizes a
compression technique to reduce the size of prompts,
resulting in faster inference and cost savings. This
project has the potential to make newer, larger
```

language models more affordable and efficient, making it a popular topic among AI enthusiasts and researchers.

In this example, the agent has decided to first translate the question into English and then use the YouTube query system you built in Listing 4.1 to gather more context before finally returning an answer.

Optimizing LLM Inference with Experiment Management

You've now spent the better part of a chapter implementing various techniques for improved LLM inference. While this is interesting in and of itself, you might be wondering how it connects to LLMOps. In this section, you'll tie everything you've learned so far together in the context of LLMOps and machine learning engineering.

Looking at everything you've implemented so far, you should have a sense of just how complex and varied the different approaches to LLM inference are. Even after you select an approach, there are an infinite number of ways you might implement it! If you think of your prompts as hyperparameters to be tuned, the possible combinations you could try are endless.

And so, you need a structured way to experiment with your LLMs, testing different prompts and parameters until you find an optimal combination for your particular task. To explore this, you'll be implementing a simple code generating assistant. In the process of doing so, you'll be optimizing your token usage (to save on cost), your prompting strategy, and some additional parameters, like the temperature argument.

The first thing you'll need is a way to log your prompts and inferences. In these examples, you'll be using Comet ML, a popular experiment management platform. As of the time of this book's writing, Comet is an industry-standard tool that is free for individual users and academics. Comet also offers paid tiers for larger teams who require more advanced features, support for larger organizations, model monitoring, or on-premise deployments, but nothing you do in this book will require a paid account. It provides everything you'll need in terms of logging, analytics, and reproducibility, and its API is simple enough that switching to a different library will be simple, if you'd like to.

Machine learning is in many ways a search problem. Given a task, you are constantly searching for the right model, the right parameters, the right dataset, etc., to achieve the highest performance possible. While exploratory data analysis and strong theoretical foundations will help you narrow the scope of your search, there is no getting away from the fact that you'll have to do quite a bit of trial and error to find the best combination for your task. It is essential, therefore, that you conduct this experimentation in a structured, reproducible way.

Years ago, the majority of data science teams were using spreadsheets and other ad hoc systems to record the results of their experiments (this is still sadly not uncommon). Code was almost never versioned via something like Git nor were models or datasets. When a model performed best, there was rarely any real certainty about exactly why or what changes led to the improvement in performance. An attitude of "don't touch it or it'll break!" often formed around successful models as a result.

Over the last several years, tools like Comet have emerged specifically for this purpose. By default, they do things like version your code, record your system details, preserve the lineage

(continued)

(continued)

of your datasets and models, and integrate with popular ML frameworks to record extra details. They also provide tools for visualizations, collaboration, and more. It is now industry standard to use these tools, as they make it easy not only to debug your models but to work in tandem with other data scientists without the fear of being unable to reproduce each other's work.

The second thing you'll need to improve your inference pipeline is a metric to optimize. With LLMs, this is a tricky task. Many of the traditional natural language processing metrics, like Recall-Oriented Understudy for Gisting Evaluation (ROUGE) scores, are just too simple in their heuristics to accurately score LLMs. ROUGE is a set of metrics used to evaluate the quality of automatic summarization systems. There are multiple variations, including ROUGE-N, ROUGE-L, ROUGE-W, and more. One of the best approaches research teams have taken recently is to use humans as direct evaluators, but this too creates problems, not the least of which is the associated cost of manually scoring samples.

Because of this, most researchers are stuck implementing custom scoring functions for their particular task, often combining different metrics like BERTScore, ROUGE, and custom benchmarks. With code generation, you have the advantage of being able to use unit tests to evaluate whether the code works, and that is exactly what you'll be doing in this next exercise.

Your task is to build a pipeline that, given a description of a Python function and some associated unit tests, will generate an acceptable piece of code.

To test your pipeline, you'll use the following prompt template:

Machine Learning Upgrade

```
code_gen_template = """#INSTRUCTION:
Write a Python function named {name} that
{description}. Make sure to include all necessary
imports.
#RESPONSE
"""

code_gen_template_w_tests = """#INSTRUCTION:
Write a Python function named {name} that
{description}. Make sure to include all necessary
imports.
The function {name} will be evaluated with the
following unit tests:
{tests}
#RESPONSE
"""
```

You'll also need some prompts and associated unit tests. The full code for the unit tests is available at this book's GitHub, but in general, the unit tests look like this:

```
class TestGenerateImage(unittest.TestCase):
    def test_valid_input(self):
        width, height = 200, 300
        image = generate_image(f'{width}x{height}')
        self.assertEqual(image.size, (width, height))
```

They are accompanied by a variable containing all of the code for the unit tests as a string. You can store all of this information, along with your prompts, in a list like so:

```
TESTS = [
    {
        "name": "generate_image(dimensions)",
```

```
            "description": "takes a string containing the
dimensions of an image, like '200x300', and generates
an image of those dimensions using 3 random colors,
before finally returning the image object.",
            "tests": image_tests,
            "tests_class": TestGenerateImage
    },
    {

            "name": "evaluate_expression(expression)",
            "description": "takes a string containing a
mathematical equation, parses the equation, and
returns its evaluated result.",
            "tests": math_tests,
            "tests_class": TestEvaluateExpression
    },
    {

            "name": "merge_k_lists(lists)",
            "description": "takes an array of k linked-
lists lists, each sorted in ascending order, and
merges all the linked-lists into one sorted linked-
list, returning the final sorted linked-list.",
            "test": merge_k_tests,
            "tests_class": TestMergeKLists
    }
]
```

Now, to perform inference, you'll need a pipeline, including nodes for your prompt and for evaluating your output, as shown in Listing 4.3.

Listing 4.3 Performing Inference with a Pipeline

```
class PromptWithMKwargsNode(Node):
    def __init__(self, prompt_template,
generate=get_completion):
```

```python
        self.prompt_template = prompt_template
        self.generate = generate
        self.prompt = None
        self.prompt_kwargs = None
    def forward(self, model_kwargs=None,
prompt_kwargs=None):
        self.prompt_kwargs = prompt_kwargs
        if self.prompt_kwargs != None:
            self.prompt = self.prompt_template.
format(**self.prompt_kwargs)
        else:
            self.prompt = self.prompt_template
        if model_kwargs != None:
            return self.generate(self.prompt, return_
full=True, **model_kwargs)
        else:
            return self.generate(self.prompt,
return_full=True)


class ExecNode(Node):
    def __init__(self):
        self.success = True
        self.message = None


    def forward(self, code):
        print(code)
        compiled = compile(code, 'test', 'exec')
        try:
            exec(compiled)
        except Exception as e:
            self.success = False
            self.message = e
            pass
```

```
            return self.success

class EvaluateNode(Node):
    def __init__(self, test_case):
        self.test_case = test_case
        self.success = False
        self.message = None
        self.results = None
    def forward(self, code):
        try:
            compiled = compile(code, 'test', 'exec')
            exec(compiled, None, globals())
        except Exception as e:
            self.success = False
            self.message = e
            return False

        test_suite = unittest.defaultTestLoader.
loadTestsFromTestCase(self.test_case)
        self.results = unittest.TextTestRunner().
run(test_suite)
        self.success = self.results.wasSuccessful()
        return self.success

class CodeGenPipeline(Pipeline):
    def __init__(self, prompt_template, test_case):
        self.p1 =
PromptWithMKwargsNode(prompt_template=prompt_template)
        self.eval = EvaluateNode(test_case=test_case)
        self.code = None
        self.model_output = None
        self.success = False
    def run(self, model_kwargs=None,
prompt_kwargs=None):
```

```python
        # Intialize your Comet Experiment
        experiment = comet_ml.Experiment(workspace=
"ckaiser", project_name="llmops-test")
        experiment.add_tag("code-gen")
        # Run pipeline
        self.model_output = self.p1.forward(model_
kwargs=model_kwargs, prompt_kwargs=prompt_kwargs)
        self.code = self.model_output.choices[0].text
        self.success = self.eval.forward(self.code)
        # Log metrics, parameters, and extra
data to Comet
        metrics = {
            "success": self.success,
            "token_usage": self.model_output.usage.
total_tokens
        }
        params = {
            "with_tests": self.p1.prompt_template ==
code_gen_template_w_tests,
            **model_kwargs
        }
        metadata = {
            "name": self.p1.prompt_kwargs['name'],
            "description": self.p1.prompt_kwargs
['description'],
            "tests": self.p1.prompt_kwargs['tests'],
            "prompt": self.p1.prompt,
            "prompt_template": self.p1.prompt_
template,
            "usage.prompt_tokens": self.model_output.
usage.prompt_tokens,
            "usage.completion_tokens": self.model_
output.usage.completion_tokens,
```

```
        "usage.total_tokens": self.model_output.
usage.total_tokens,
        }
        experiment.log_metrics(metrics)
        experiment.log_parameters(params)
        experiment.log_others(metadata)
        return self.success
```

Think about what you want out of a system like this. It's important for it to produce runnable code, yes, but you also want to minimize the amount you spend on API calls. So, you want to maximize the overall effectiveness of the pipeline but minimize its total token usage.

There are many strategies you may try and parameters you might tune to optimize for this goal, and you are encouraged to experiment further, but in this exercise, you're going to focus on just a handful. You are going to experiment with the length of the context you pass your model and with your temperature parameter. The results of each experiment will be logged to Comet, and you will be able to evaluate which combination maximized the quality of your code while minimizing the total number of tokens used.

The following code will structure and run your experiments:

```
for test in TESTS:
    for template in [code_gen_template,
code_gen_template_w_tests]:
        for temperature in [0.0, 0.5, 1.0, 1.5]:
            model_kwargs = { "temperature": temp }
            pipeline = CodeGenPipeline(prompt_
template=template, test_case=test['tests_class'])
            success = pipeline.run(model_kwargs=model_
kwargs, prompt_kwargs=test)
```

This process will systematically try different combinations of temperatures and prompts. You can then visualize your results from within Comet itself through the Comet site, or via the Comet API.

We've covered a lot in this section, and yet, we've just scratched the surface of the field of prompt engineering. There are many parameters besides temperature that you might explore. If you decide to try tuning multiple parameters, consider using an open-source library like Optuna, as they've simplified the task of hyperparameter tuning greatly. Additionally, there are more and more techniques being formalized every day for optimizing prompts. Projects like Microsoft's LLMLingua, for example, use smaller language models to compress and optimize context, claiming as much as 20x improvements in efficiency with minimal performance loss.

Whatever you decide to do, the important thing to take away from this section is that LLM inference is not a magical process that relies solely on your intuition and tinkering. You can, and should, approach it as an optimization problem, applying a structured, engineer-like mindset to the task.

Fine-Tuning LLMs

So far, you've thoroughly explored all the ways you can improve the performance of your LLM without introducing any extra training. The obvious next step is to explore how you can improve performance *with* some extra training. In this section, you're going to explore fine-tuning as a strategy for improving performance on specific tasks.

By the end of this section, you should feel comfortable deciding whether or not to fine-tune a model, and further, you should have a good grasp of how to go about fine-tuning in an efficient manner.

When to Fine-Tune an LLM

A more standard treatment of large language models might begin with fine-tuning before addressing prompt engineering or any of the topics that have been covered so far. This book, however, uses an applied, production-focused lens for viewing LLMs. With that framing, fine-tuning should be the last thing you explore, as it requires the most up-front investment in terms of both pure cost and engineering time.

Whereas prompt engineering experiments can be run fairly quickly and at low cost, to fine-tune a model you must collect a dataset, write training code, configure a system for evaluation, provision the necessary compute resources, and typically run multiple experiments to find a successful model.

All of these steps require a nontrivial effort and investment, but there are some situations where the investment is worth it. Broadly, you can categorize these situations in two groups:

- **Fine-tuning as an optimization.** Techniques like RAG and agentic approaches use more tokens and are therefore, more expensive and slower. When you've maximized improvements in your model via prompt engineering techniques, it is often worth it to "bake in" some of those techniques to your model via fine-tuning, such that your model no longer needs to generate as many tokens to arrive at its final answer.

- **Fine-tuning for domain-specific tasks.** In some cases, you may be dealing with a task that requires not just domain-specific knowledge but domain-specific behavior. For example, there may be a "tone" you need your model to write with or a format that you need your output in. In these situations, fine-tuning is necessary to train your model to adapt these specific behaviors, while in-context learning solutions (like RAG) provide the model with the specific knowledge it needs.

Now, regardless of your reasons for fine-tuning, you are going to have to solve one obvious problem: large language models are large. Especially in training, they eat expensive compute resources in huge quantities. Training a 1 trillion parameter model like GPT-4 is simply unrealistic, unless you have an enormous budget.

However, there are many strategies for performing training (and inference) more efficiently, on cheaper hardware. Let's explore some of these techniques.

Quantization, QLOrA, and Parameter Efficient Fine-Tuning

In this section, you'll fine-tune a 7 billion parameter model using nothing more than a T4 GPU with 14 GB of VRAM. At the time of this book's writing, such a GPU is offered for free by platforms like Google Colab.

To achieve this, the first problem you need to solve is simply downloading the model and loading it into memory. While "small" by contemporary standards, 7 billion parameter models still routinely require more than 15 GB of VRAM. To get around this limitation, you're going to use one of the most efficient 7 billion parameter models, and you're going to further reduce its compute footprint by quantizing it down to a smaller size.

Quantization is a technique employed to reduce the model's memory footprint. Historically, the concept of quantization has roots in digital signal processing, where it was used to reduce the bit representation of multimedia data to save storage space and bandwidth. As neural networks grew in size and complexity, there was a commensurate increase in attempts to adapt quantization techniques to models.

(continued)

113

(continued)

Quantization in the context of LLMs involves reducing the precision of the model's parameters from floating-point representations (typically 32 bits) to lower bit depths, such as 16, 8, or even fewer bits. This reduction not only decreases the model size, making it more accessible for deployment on devices with limited memory, but also speeds up computation, as operations on lower-precision numbers are faster on specialized hardware.

Quantized models lose some of the expressivity of "full" models, but there has been quite a bit of research into maximizing the compression of quantized models while minimizing the drop in model quality. Now, many LLMs can be run on consumer hardware with very good results thanks to quantization.

You can follow along with the code in this section a bit more easily by following the notebook titled 04_05_fine_tuning in this book's GitHub repository. You can find a more robust implementation of QLoRA on the official QLoRA GitHub repository at `https://github.com/artidoro/qlora`.

The first thing you'll need to do is install some dependencies.

```
$ pip install -q -U trl accelerate git+https://github
.com/huggingface/peft.git git+https://github.com/
huggingface/transformers.git
$ pip install -q datasets bitsandbytes comet-ml
```

Most of these are Hugging Face libraries used for training language models. The two exceptions are Comet ML, which you've previously used for experiment tracking, and BitsAndBytes, which is a library for quantizing models.

Once you've installed your dependencies, you'll need to download your dataset. You can do this using Hugging Face's datasets library. In particular, you'll be using the Guanaco dataset, which is a subset of the popular OpenAssistant dataset.

```
from datasets import load_dataset
dataset_name = "timdettmers/openassistant-guanaco"
dataset = load_dataset(dataset_name, split="train")
```

Now, you can initialize your model. In this project, you'll be using a 7 billion parameter, instruction-tuned model from Mistral. At the time of this book's writing, this model is one of the more remarkable achievements in open-source machine learning. The model performs at a level comparable to many significantly larger models despite its small size, including on general reasoning tasks. Being smaller, you can run the model on cheaper GPUs and can even fine-tune it.

> The Mistral 7B[10] model, released by Mistral AI, is a 7.3 billion parameter language model that surpasses the performance of Llama 2 13B across all benchmarks and matches or exceeds Llama 1 34B on many. It approaches the performance of CodeLlama 7B on coding tasks while maintaining proficiency in English.

(continued)

---

[10]Albert Q. Jiang, Alexandre Sablayrolles, Arthur Mensch, Chris Bamford, Devendra Singh Chaplot, Diego de las Casas, Florian Bressand, Gianna Lengyel, Guillaume Lample, Lucile Saulnier, Lélio Renard Lavaud, Marie-Anne Lachaux, Pierre Stock, Teven Le Scao, Thibaut Lavril, Thomas Wang, Timothée Lacroix, and William El Sayed, "Mistral 7B", October 2023, arXiv, https://arxiv.org/abs/2310.06825

(continued)

> The model, which is open-source, uses several optimizations to self-attention to improve efficiency in training and inference. In addition, the model was fine-tuned for instruction following, resulting in a model named Mistral 7B Instruct, which outperforms all other 7B models and is comparable with most 13B chat models.

Run the following code to initialize your model:

```
import torch
from transformers import AutoModelForCausalLM,
AutoTokenizer, BitsAndBytesConfig
model_name = "mistralai/Mistral-7B-v0.1"
bnb_config = BitsAndBytesConfig(
    load_in_4bit=True,
    bnb_4bit_use_double_quant=True,
    bnb_4bit_quant_type="nf4",
    bnb_4bit_compute_dtype=torch.bfloat16,
)
model = AutoModelForCausalLM.from_pretrained(
    model_name,
    quantization_config=bnb_config,
)
model.config.use_cache = False
tokenizer = AutoTokenizer.from_pretrained(model_name,
trust_remote_code=True)
tokenizer.pad_token = tokenizer.eos_token
```

Now, you're almost ready to fine-tune your model. There is, however, one modification you need to make before your model is ready. Namely, we need to set up some LoRA adapters.

Low-rank adaptation (LoRA)[11] is an approach to more efficiently fine-tune the training of large language models. At its core, LoRA allows for the efficient tuning of pretrained LLMs by adapting only a small portion of the model's parameters, rather than the entire model. This is achieved by introducing trainable low-rank matrices that adjust the pre-existing weights of the model's layers. The key insight behind LoRA is that these small, additional matrices can capture the necessary adjustments to the model's behavior for a specific task, without requiring modifications to the original, much larger set of weights. This methodology significantly reduces the computational resources and time required for training, making the adaptation of LLMs more accessible and sustainable.

For machine learning practitioners, the appeal of LoRA lies in its balance between efficiency and performance. By fine-tuning only a fraction of the model's parameters, LoRA maintains or even enhances the model's performance on specific tasks, while drastically reducing the computational cost associated with traditional full-model fine-tuning. This efficiency opens up new possibilities for applying LLMs across a wider range of applications and industries, especially those with limited access to computational resources. Furthermore, LoRA's approach to maintaining the bulk of the pretrained model untouched means that the foundational knowledge captured during pretraining is preserved, ensuring that the adapted model benefits from the general capabilities of the LLM while being customized for particular needs.

---

[11]Edward J. Hu, Yelong Shen, Phillip Wallis, Zeyuan Allen-Zhu, Yuanzhi Li, Shean Wang, Lu Wang, and Weizhu Chen, "LoRA: Low-Rank Adaptation of Large Language Models", June 2021, arXiv, `https://arxiv.org/abs/2106.09685`

Standing Up Your LLM

The following code will configure your LoRA adapters:

```
from peft import LoraConfig
lora_alpha = 16
lora_dropout = 0.1
lora_r = 64
peft_config = LoraConfig(
    lora_alpha=lora_alpha,
    lora_dropout=lora_dropout,
    r=lora_r,
    bias="none",
    task_type="CAUSAL_LM",
    target_modules=[
        "q_proj",
        "k_proj",
        "v_proj",
        "gate_proj",
        "up_proj",
        "down_proj",
    ]
)
```

Now that your adapters are in place, you can begin fine-tuning. In Listing 4.4, you use the Hugging Face Trainer to manage your training loop. One of the many conveniences of this utility is that it integrates with Comet automatically, meaning that your training runs will be tracked and managed without any additional boilerplate code on your part (though, of course, you are encouraged to experiment with logging additional parameters and metrics).

Listing 4.4   Fine-Tuning Code

```
from transformers import TrainingArguments
from trl import SFTTrainer
```

```python
import comet_ml
comet_ml.init(project_name="finetune-mistral7b")
output_dir = "./results"
per_device_train_batch_size = 4
gradient_accumulation_steps = 4
optim = "paged_adamw_32bit"
save_steps = 10
logging_steps = 10
learning_rate = 2e-4
max_grad_norm = 0.3
max_steps = 500
warmup_ratio = 0.03
lr_scheduler_type = "constant"
training_arguments = TrainingArguments(
    output_dir=output_dir,
    per_device_train_batch_size=per_device_
train_batch_size,
    gradient_accumulation_steps=gradient_
accumulation_steps,
    optim=optim,
    save_steps=save_steps,
    logging_steps=logging_steps,
    learning_rate=learning_rate,
    fp16=True,
    max_grad_norm=max_grad_norm,
    max_steps=max_steps,
    warmup_ratio=warmup_ratio,
    group_by_length=False,
    lr_scheduler_type=lr_scheduler_type,
    gradient_checkpointing=True,
)
max_seq_length = 512
trainer = SFTTrainer(
    model=model,
```

Standing Up Your LLM

```
        train_dataset=dataset,
        peft_config=peft_config,
        dataset_text_field="text",
        max_seq_length=max_seq_length,
        tokenizer=tokenizer,
        args=training_arguments,
        packing=True,
)
trainer.train()
```

And now, if you look in your Comet dashboard, you will see your loss steadily decreasing as you train (see Figure 4.6).

You are encouraged to experiment with this project. Try using a different dataset, or even a different model, and see what results you can generate.

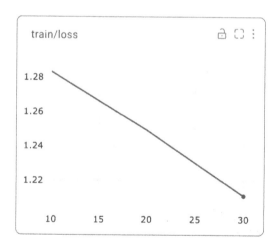

Figure 4.6 Tracking training runs with Comet

Wrapping Things Up

This has been a hefty chapter. You learned all about performing inference on an LLM, including prompt engineering for optimal outputs, model quantization, and how to fine-tune an LLM.

Every week it seems, new techniques are discovered for improved model training. Within a year of this book's publication, there may be 3 billion parameter models capable of matching today's 30 billion parameter models. With that in mind, your goal in reading this chapter and completing the exercises shouldn't be to memorize every neat trick in training and inference. You should strive to feel a general familiarity with the "flavors," for lack of a better word, of approaches to training and inference. With this foundation in place, you'll be able to pick up new developments in the field quickly.

Putting Together an Application

In previous chapters, you've written scripts and notebooks to apply models to problems. You've learned to version your data and track your experiments. You've learned more than enough to solve real, meaningful problems with machine learning and large language models, in particular. The next obvious question is: "How do you build something other people can use?" There are a couple of different options, like building a dashboard, an application programming interface (API), or making the model available through a command-line interface.

You'll need to decide what "production" means to you in a particular instance to determine what flavor of production is the right move. It's important to consider who the end user is, what they expect regarding a deliverable, and the best way to deliver on those expectations. This may involve considering the type of inference required to meet those expectations. What kind of pipeline do you need to perform that inference? What kind of deployment can support that pipeline? Dashboards will likely have the least infrastructure requirements, while a real-time API will be more demanding.

Here, we've decided to demonstrate both a dashboard and an API. If these options are new to you, here are some items you might want to consider when deciding how to serve up your model to end users. The benefits of creating a dashboard include the following:

- **User-friendly interface:** If the target audience is nontechnical, prefers visual representations, and needs an intuitive interface to interact with the model's outcomes, a dashboard might be the right move.

- **Real-time monitoring:** If the model's predictions or results need constant monitoring or reporting by the end user, a dashboard provides a live view of changing data.

Alternatively, you might be thinking that an API is more appropriate for your project. In that case, the main benefits of deploying a model as an API are as follows:

- **Automated access and integration:**
  - **Programmatic access:** APIs enable programmatic access to the model's predictions, facilitating seamless integration into other applications, systems, or workflows.
  - **Scalability:** APIs are ideal for handling high traffic and scaling to accommodate a large number of requests.
- **Backend interactions:**
  - **Backend processes:** If the primary use case involves backend processes, automated tasks, or integration into existing systems, an API is preferable.
  - **Streamlined workflow:** APIs facilitate automation and streamline workflows by allowing systems to communicate and share data without a graphical interface.
- **Developer-Friendly:**
  - **Developer focus:** APIs are developer-friendly and can attract a technical audience looking to integrate machine learning functionality into their applications or services.

- **Flexibility:** APIs offer flexibility in how users interact with and leverage the model's capabilities programmatically.

As mentioned, these two different approaches largely depend on the end user and how they'll be using the dashboard or API. Here are some of the elements you'll be considering:

- **User needs:** Understand the preferences and requirements of the end users or systems interacting with the model's outputs.

- **Usability versus automation:** Determine whether the primary need is user interaction and visualization or automated access and integration.

- **Scalability:** Consider the anticipated volume of usage and the model's potential future growth.

- **Resource constraints:** Evaluate available resources, time, expertise, and infrastructure for development and maintenance.

After you've considered your options and needs, you might find that it's time to build an app. In the next section, we'll be using Gradio.

Prototyping with Gradio

We'd like to get you up and running quickly, so this first pass will be setting up a simple app, and then we'll add a drop-down selector, a tab, a download button, and some other elements later. First, take a look at what your first-iteration, finished Gradio app will look like (see Figure 5.1).

You'll see in Figure 5.1 that you have a place for the end user to enter their query. Then, you'll be returned the relevant pieces of text so that you can inspect the output that is driving the displayed visualization. You'll also have the histogram that displays the title of a video and how many relevant chunks of text were in the description. The length of the chunks of text is variable; there is potential overlap

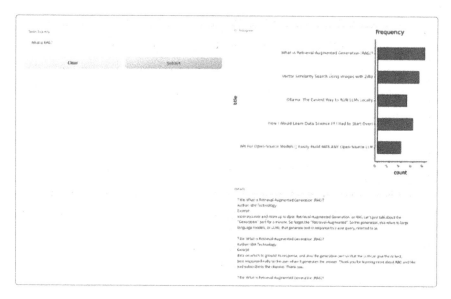

Figure 5.1 Prototype using Gradio

in the pieces of text, and some videos are much longer than others. The histogram is a very "rough" metric for assessing how relevant a video is, and certainly isn't the most scientific measurement to ever grace a book, but it should be more than enough to illustrate the process of prototyping with Gradio.

Building an app with a user interface is one way to make your application valuable, usable, and available to others. Many app frameworks exist besides Gradio, including Shiny (in Python and R), Streamlit, and others. These app frameworks allow you to create a user-friendly, interactive interface and deploy machine learning models without in-depth knowledge of web development. These frameworks have a number of similarities in common:

- **Abstraction:** These frameworks abstract away the complexities of web development, allowing users to focus on defining the application logic and UI components.

- **Reactivity:** They leverage reactive programming paradigms, automatically updating the UI based on changes in inputs or variables.

- **Backend integration:** They simplify the integration of back-end functionalities (machine learning models, data processing, etc.) with the UI, making it easier to create interactive applications.

Gradio supports a wide array of input types, from text and images to audio and video. Similarly, it facilitates varied outputs, enabling the presentation of results through text, images, plots, and audio. Developers and users can personalize interfaces by modifying layouts, styles, and components, tailoring the app to specific preferences or branding requirements.

Gradio's live code editing feature facilitates instant updates to the interface, providing immediate feedback during development. Additionally, it simplifies sharing applications via shareable links or embed codes, enabling easy deployment and distribution. Seamless integration with various machine learning frameworks allows users to deploy models developed with TensorFlow, PyTorch, scikit-learn, etc. Its interoperability extends beyond Python, facilitating integration with models developed in other languages or frameworks. Gradio enables interactive data exploration, fostering data-driven insights through visual representations. Users can receive immediate predictions or feedback from machine learning models, aiding decision-making or exploring hypothetical scenarios.

The beauty of these frameworks is that they're becoming delightful to work with. The Python code is often straightforward (although we all have rough days), and it takes only a few lines of code to get an app up and running.

Before we get started with the app, we'll still need to create the visual that we plan to display on the app. Gradio does not support

Plotnine, the visualization library that we'll be using, but here we will create a graphic, store it as an image, and then display it on the dashboard. When a new user query is entered, a new plot will be created, saved, and displayed. The systematic approach of the *Grammar of Graphics* by Leland Wilkinson (Springer, 2005) that is leveraged in Plotnine fits well in a book where we're talking about operations.

Creating Graphics with Plotnine

Plotnine, a Python library inspired by ggplot2 in R, empowers users to create elegant and expressive visualizations, leveraging the *Grammar of Graphics*. It's a way of thinking about and constructing visualizations, providing a structured approach to creating graphics by breaking them down into fundamental components. The following are the core elements of Wilkinson's *Grammar of Graphics*:

- **Aesthetic mappings (**`aes`**):** Aesthetic mappings link variables in the dataset to visual properties such as color, size, shape, and position. These mappings define how data attributes are represented visually, such as mapping a variable to the x-axis or color gradient.

- **Geometric objects (**`geom`**):** Geoms are the visual elements used to represent data points in a plot. Examples include `geom_point()` for scatterplots and `geom_bar()` for bar charts.

- **Scaling:** The x- and y-axes are used. Should the axes of our visual be represented as decimals, percentages, log, etc., then scaling will help you handle this.

- **Labs:** This is where you'll define your labels, including main title, axis labels, legend title, subtitle, caption, etc.

- **Faceting:** Faceting involves splitting the dataset into subsets and creating multiple plots, each displaying a subset of the data. It helps visualize different segments of data simultaneously.

Beyond these concrete attributes, the *Grammar of Graphics* is driven by a few core ideas.

- **Breakdown of visualization:** The *Grammar of Graphics* breaks down the process of visualization into modular components. Each component (data, aesthetic mapping, geoms, etc.) contributes to the creation of the final graphic.
- **Layering:** Visualizations are built by layering different components on top of each other. For instance, multiple geoms (points, lines) can be layered to create complex visual representations.
- **Flexibility and consistency:** The grammar allows for flexibility in creating various visualizations while maintaining a consistent and coherent structure. Users can modify specific components to change the visualization without restructuring the plot.
- **Customization:** The grammar facilitates customization by allowing users to tweak aesthetic mappings, geoms, scales, and other components to achieve the desired visualization.

With all of this in mind, you can begin building your plot.

```
from plotnine import (
    ggplot,
    geom_histogram,
    aes,
    theme,
    element_text,
    labs,
    coord_flip
)
```

```
from plotnine.themes.theme_classic import
theme_classic
    # creating a list of the titles to make a
dataframe for the histogram
    titles = []
    for result in results[0]:
        titles.append(
            [result['entity']['title']])
    # at this point, titles will look like:
    # [ ['Beginner - Data Science'], ['Beginner -
Data Science'], ['20 Quick Tips'] ]
    # plotnine needs a dataframe!
    titles_dataframe = pd.DataFrame(data=titles,
columns=['title'])
    p = ggplot(titles_dataframe, aes(x='title')) + \
    geom_histogram(binwidth=0.5,
                        colour="#000000",
                        fill='#ff007f',
                        position="identity") + \
    coord_flip() + \
    theme_classic() + \
    theme(axis_text_x=element_text(rotation=45,
hjust=1)) + \
    labs(title='Frequency of Relevant Text Chunks')
```

Great, we have our plot and our vector database set up and ready to go. We still have a bit of data cleanup to get this into the format we'll need to display on our app. Since we want to see the associated text output of the data for the graph going into our app, we'll need to set that up. Again, there is a Colab added to the *Machine Learning Upgrade* GitHub so that all you'll need to do is run the code provided.

First, we can easily create an image of our plot, and then we'll pass the name of the image to Gradio.

```
image_name = 'image.png'
p.save(image_name)
```

Next, we need to build a string with the information we'd like to have in our output on the app.

```
output_text = "
    for result in results[0]:
       output_text += 'Title: ' + result['entity']
['title'] + '\n'
       output_text += 'Author: ' + result['entity']
['author'] + '\n'
       output_text += 'Excerpt:\n' + result['entity']
['text'] + '\n\n'
```

The previous two elements are part of a function called `search_video_parts`; this function is passed to Gradio. We wrote this so that if your database is already set up, you can import your libraries, run the function, and display the app. If you still need to set up the vector database, you must do that first (see Chapter 3, "A Data-Centric View"). The following code cannot be run stand-alone but is part of a larger function in the GitHub repo; however, we wanted to be able to walk you through this code piece by piece for clarity. Finally, you'll be able to display the app with the following code:

```
demo = gr.Interface(
    fn=search_video_parts, # This is the function
defined earlier in this block.
    inputs=gr.Textbox(label="Search query"),
    outputs= [
```

```
        gr.Image(label="histogram"), # The first thing
returned is an image name
        gr.Textbox(label="details") # The second thing
returned is a string
    ]
)
demo.launch(debug=True)
```

gr.Interface() is the core function used to create the user
interface. It takes in a machine learning model or a function, along
with various optional parameters, to define the inputs, outputs, and
UI components. inputs specifies the type of input the user interacts
with, such as text, image, video, or a combination thereof. It allows
defining the input format and constraints. outputs specifies the
type of output the user receives after interacting with the model, and
launch() launches the Gradio interface on a local server, enabling
users to interact with the defined model or function through a web
interface.

You'll first pip install your dependencies and restart your runtime
(click Runtime and then Restart Session). The installs looks like this:

```
!pip install \
  pymilvus==2.3.4 \
  langchain==0.0.352 \
  openai==1.6.1 \
  pytube==15.0.0 \
  youtube-transcript-api==0.6.1 \
  pyarrow==14.0.2 \
  typing_extensions==4.9.0 \  gradio
```

Now the code shown in Listing 5.1 will create your app.

Listing 5.1 Creating an App with Gradio and Plotnine

```python
import gradio as gr
import openai
import pandas as pd
from plotnine import (
    ggplot,
    geom_histogram,
    aes,
    theme,
    element_text,
    labs,
    coord_flip
)

from plotnine.themes.theme_classic import
theme_classic
from pymilvus import (
    Collection,
    CollectionSchema,
    connections,
    DataType,
    FieldSchema,
    utility,
    MilvusClient
)

COLLECTION_NAME = 'youtube'
ZILLIZ_CLUSTER_URI = '[YOUR_ZILLIZ_URI]'
# Endpoint URI obtained from Zilliz Cloud
ZILLIZ_API_KEY = '[YOUR_ZILLIZ_API_KEY]'
```

```
connections.connect(uri=ZILLIZ_CLUSTER_URI,
token=ZILLIZ_API_KEY, secure=True)

client = MilvusClient(
    uri=ZILLIZ_CLUSTER_URI,
    token=ZILLIZ_API_KEY)

openai_client = openai.OpenAI(api_key=
'[YOUR_OPENAI_API_KEY]'

# Extract embedding from text using OpenAI
string -> vector
# This function is directly from https://docs.zilliz
.com/docs/similarity-search-with-zilliz-cloud-and-
openai, but with "text-embedding-ada-002" added.
def create_embedding_from_string(text):
    return openai_client.embeddings.create(
        input=text,
        model='text-embedding-ada-002').data[0]
.embedding

def search_video_parts(query):

    results = client.search(
      collection_name=COLLECTION_NAME,
      data=[create_embedding_from_string(query)],
# Embeded search value
      search_params={ "metric_type": "IP" },
      limit=30,  # Limit to 30 results per search
      output_fields=['title', 'author', 'part_id',
'max_part_id', 'text'])  # Include title
field in result

    # creating a list of the titles to make a
dataframe for the histogram
```

```
titles = []
for result in results[0]:
  titles.append(
      [result['entity']['title']])
# at this point, titles will look like:
# [ ['Beginner - Data Science'], ['Beginner -
Data Science'], ['20 Quick Tips'] ]

# plotnine needs a dataframe!
titles_dataframe = pd.DataFrame(data=titles,
columns=['title'])

p = ggplot(titles_dataframe, aes(x='title')) + \
  geom_histogram(binwidth=0.5,
                 colour="#000000",
                 fill='#ff007f',
                 position="identity") + \
  coord_flip() + \
  theme_classic() + \
  theme(axis_text_x=element_text(rotation=45,
hjust=1)) + \
  labs(title='Frequency of Relevant Text Chunks')

# Save the plot to an image and call it "image
.png" Return this image name to gradio
image_name = 'image.png'
p.save(image_name)

# Build a string with lots of info from the
search response
output_text = ''
for result in results[0]:
  output_text += 'Title: ' + result['entity']
['title'] + '\n'
```

```
    output_text += 'Author: ' + result['entity']
['author'] + '\n'
    output_text += 'Excerpt:\n' + result['entity']
['text'] + '\n\n'


    # Return multiple values, which gradio can display
in separate boxes
    return image_name, output_text

demo = gr.Interface(
    fn=search_video_parts, # This is the function
defined earlier in this block.
    inputs=gr.Textbox(label="Search query"),
    outputs= [
        gr.Image(label="histogram"), # The first thing
returned is an image name
        gr.Textbox(label="details")  # The second
thing returned is a string
    ]
)


demo.launch(debug=True)
```

This is exciting; you now have a working app! It feels awesome to have a working app. However, there is obviously a lot missing here. In the real world, you'll probably want to add drop-down selectors, a table, additional rows, or custom CSS to adjust the look and feel. This will not be a full overview of Gradio, but we'll cover a little more to help you on your way.

- Adding a drop-down selector for the author

- Adding a logo

- Creating a tab to put the "details window" on the new tab

Figure 5.2 Gradio app with more features

- Adding a title and subtitle to the top left of the UI
- Changing the color of the buttons
- Creating a Click To Download button
- Putting it all together

We've found that these items are often some of the first features mentioned for a UI when a client is looking to have an app built. You'll want to make sure that the first couple of cells of the notebook have already been run and you're connected to the database before executing these code blocks. Figure 5.2 shows a slightly more built-out view of the dashboard.

Here, the tabs allow you to show the histogram, the details, or a button to download the data. Whether your app is for BI or AI, don't be surprised if your stakeholders ask for that download button.

Adding the Author Selector

When working on a more complex project, your end users are often going to have data elements that they'll want to be able to filter on in the dashboard. Since our dataset isn't very complex, the example we used was a drop-down selector for the author. To add this to your app, you'll use the drop-down function. This will add the drop-down to the UI, but it is not hooked up yet.

Figure 5.3 Adding the author selector

```
with gr.Blocks() as app:
  gr.Textbox(label="Search query")
  gr.Dropdown(value="Kristen Kehrer",
choices=["Kristen Kehrer", "Ken Jee"],
interactive=True)

app.launch(debug=True)
```

Now you have a drop-down, as you can see in Figure 5.3.

As shown in Figure 5.3, we added only the *aesthetic* of a drop-down; there is no submit button. When you see the final code working together, you'll also add the author in the `submit.click` function to make this work.

```
submit.click(fn=search_video_parts,
             inputs=[query, author],
             outputs=[hist, details, download])
```

Adding a Logo

We are going to use a URL for the Data Moves Me logo and add this to our app. In Gradio, *blocks* typically refer to the components used to build, create, and customize a user interface. Here we are using an HTML function in Gradio for passing the logo and using a bit of styling to customize the width of the image, the background color, and how much padding is used. Although this code runs, there is not much to see here. We're merely rendering the Data Moves Me logo.

```
LOGO_URL = "https://images.squarespace-cdn.com/content/
v1/64d51f57b818e4765cf3b0bb/489ed659-eac3-48e2-9043-
3b653cc4d173/DATAMOVESME_COLOR.png?format=1500w"

with gr.Blocks(fill_height=True) as app:
  gr.HTML(f'<img src="{LOGO_URL}" style="width:300px;
background-color: white; padding:5px" />')

app.launch(debug=True)
```

Adding a Tab

Next, we'll add a tab. Gradio tabs are a convenient and effective way to organize and present multiple components or views within a single interface. Here, we're specifying that we'll have two tabs; the first will be a "histogram" tab that will contain an image, and the second tab will be for the associated data that was used to create the histogram. Therefore, the second tab will be a textbox, with gr.Blocks() as app.

```
    with gr.Tab('Histogram'):
      gr.Image()
    with gr.Tab('Details'):
      gr.Textbox()

app.launch(debug=True)
```

Figure 5.4 shows the tabs.

Figure 5.4   Adding tabs

Adding a Title and Subtitle

Titles and subtitles in Gradio are essential for providing context, guiding users, and enhancing the overall user experience. We'll be using another block to help customize our layout, and the HTML function to add our text. Here we're creating an h1 header and an em subheader. Em is a unit of measurement in CSS and is related to the font size of the text.

```
with gr.Blocks() as app:
  gr.HTML('<h1>An inspiring title!')
  gr.HTML('<em>Getting your stuff the way you
want it.')

app.launch(debug=True)
```

Changing the Color of the Buttons

Between adding a logo and grabbing the brand palette of your employer or client to give your dashboard a branded feel, it can be a quick way to make a demo much snazzier. Gradio has predefined colors to choose from (like our teal here), but you can also pass custom color objects to get more specific with color. The following code sets up two buttons, one for clearing the input, another for submitting it, and applies a theme with a teal color scheme.

```
theme = gr.themes.Default(primary_hue="teal")

with gr.Blocks(fill_height=True, theme=theme) as app:
  gr.Textbox(label="text")
  with gr.Row():
    gr.Button('clear')
    gr.Button('submit', variant='primary')
app.launch(debug=True)
```

Figure 5.5 Changing button color

In Figure 5.5 you should see a teal button.

Click to Download Button

The following code allows you to download the histogram image. You'll want to first ensure that you've put an image in your files named `image.png` for you to download. The file should be placed not in the `sample_data` folder in Colab, but at the same level that the `sample_data` folder is in. You'll notice on the right you can click the blue downward arrow to download it.

```
with gr.Blocks() as app:
  gr.File('image.png')

app.launch(debug=True)
```

Figure 5.6 displays your ability to now download the photo.

Figure 5.6 Adding a download button

Putting It All Together

Here is the code for the final app with the features we just covered:

```
LOGO_URL = "https://images.squarespace-cdn.com/content/
v1/64d51f57b818e4765cf3b0bb/489ed659-eac3-48e2-9043-
3b653cc4d173/DATAMOVESME_COLOR.png?format=1500w"
```

```python
query = gr.Textbox(label="Search query")
author = gr.Dropdown(label="Author",
                     value="Kristen Kehrer",
                     choices=["Kristen Kehrer",
"Ken Jee"])
hist = gr.Image(label="histogram")
details = gr.Textbox(label="details", lines=20)
submit = gr.Button("submit")
download = gr.File(label="Download results")

with gr.Blocks(fill_height=True) as app:
  gr.HTML(f'<img src="{LOGO_URL}" style="width:300px;
background-color: white; padding:5px"/>')
  gr.HTML('<h1>An inspiring title!')
  gr.HTML('<em>Getting your stuff the way you
want it.')
  with gr.Row():
    with gr.Column():
      query.render()
      author.render()
      submit.render()
    with gr.Column():
      with gr.Tab('Histogram'):
        hist.render()
      with gr.Tab('Details'):
        details.render()
      with gr.Tab('Download'):
        download.render()

    submit.click(fn=search_video_parts,
                 inputs=[query, author],
                 outputs=[hist, details, download])

app.launch(debug=True)
```

Now you've got an app with some common elements you'd be asked to incorporate by your stakeholders. Once you have a large language model–powered (LLM-powered) app demo, you might find that the latency is not good enough for you to try to roll it out as is. At this point, you won't have many concurrent users (because no one is using your app yet). Meaning, this isn't a question of just ramping up the resources, unless maybe your dataset is quite large. When first trying to improve the latency of your app, you'll see that the number of output tokens is going to be one of the biggest factors impacting the latency; the input tokens will not have as much of an impact. One fantastic article we found on the subject is at `https://www .taivo.ai/__making-gpt-api-responses-faster`.

For a use case where Kristen had to work through a latency issue (an LLM-powered app for a consultancy that would be using the tool internally, meaning small traffic). Ultimately, the solution was to make three concurrent API calls when the user hits Submit. She found that the variability in response time was quite large when running the app. One request might take a minute, and another request might take five minutes; neither response time was anything that any human would want to wait for regularly. By making three API calls and choosing the fastest to display, the latency of the app was improved by three times, but with few users, the faster output time was well worth it. At the time of writing this book and with the number of tokens involved in each API call, this would cost about 7.5 cents per use.

Other considerations were the model being used. The project started using the default model, which was GPT 3.5. When upgraded to GPT 4, it was clear the output was higher quality, but it took longer to run. In this particular use case, the quality of the content was the most important aspect, as the content would be customer facing. The application was going to be used to generate content for communications, so having great content was a necessity.

143

Putting Together an Application

Much prompt tuning went into the instructions around how the content should look and sound.

The last piece in improving the latency of the app was to reduce the number of output tokens. Originally, the output consisted of a letter and then a second output box that spoke to the reasoning involved in writing the letter. The number of output tokens was around 1,500. Part of the reduction in latency came from asking the model to reduce the number of reasons it gave for how the model created the content and to keep the output concise.

In the end, we were averaging about 20 seconds per run of the app.

Ideally, you now feel like you'd be able to build a simple LLM-powered app and understand what might impact the latency. If you've decided that your use case involves deploying an API, we discuss how to do this next.

Deploying Models as APIs

To wrap up this chapter, you're going to deploy an API that implements one of the pipelines you designed back in Chapter 4. You're going to do this both with the OpenAI API and with an LLM that you deploy to your own cloud account (though the second part is optional).

Deployment is a funny topic in machine learning. The definition of "production" varies wildly from project to project, and as a result, "deploying to production" can mean anything from generating predictions from a local model once a week to deploying a real-time API that can handle 1,000 concurrent users. In the next chapter, you'll be exploring different architectures in greater depth, but for now, you'll be focused on deploying a simple server for inference.

The general architecture of your deployment is straightforward. You'll have a user-facing API that takes requests from your application's users. Behind that, you'll have your hosted model (or OpenAIs), which your user-facing API will communicate with.

In a more complex setting, you might have many other components. For instance, a vector database would likely run as its own service, as would any other databases your application needs. You'd likely implement a real web server like NGINX to handle incoming requests, and all of these various services would probably be deployed to a *Kubernetes cluster*. However, implementing all of that is a significant infrastructure project that would typically be done by a dedicated platform engineering team.

Each of these components is a stand-alone service, with their own dedicated resources. You can think of them as each running on different computers (in a very technical sense, they may be running as different virtual machines on the same larger computer). Why is this? There are a few reasons.

First, separating your services is an effective way to control costs. These services have different computational needs. Your web server does not need much in the way of infrastructure. It can scale up to thousands of users easily with very cheap hardware. Your LLM, however, needs very powerful GPUs, which are expensive. By decoupling these services, you can scale up your GPUs as needed but keep the resources for your web server relatively low.

The second reason involves security and control. You don't want users to have direct access to your model. For example, it's reasonable to assume that you will want to impose some limit on how often a user can query your LLM. You don't want bots flooding your model with requests, racking up huge compute bills and degrading the service for real users. To implement this rate limit, you'll need your server to perform some complex logic. You'll need to log user requests and, for each query, check to see how many requests the user has made recently. Performing all of this inside the same service that runs inference on your LLM is unnecessarily complex and potentially introduces some performance slowdowns for your model, which now has to wait for the checks to complete before it can run.

Finally, and related to the previous two reasons, is the issue of improvability. Remember that you ultimately want to build systems that are improvable. Say you want to use your LLM for a different feature later, one that doesn't require the same rate limiting. You won't be able to if that rate-limiting logic is embedded in your inference API. Similarly, any feature you want to add is likely to require its own computational resources. With LLMs being as compute-hungry as they are, embedding extra services on the same machine as your LLM is ultimately going to limit its performance.

To get your hands around these concepts, the rest of this chapter will be dedicated to implementing a simple deployment, starting with the user-facing API.

Implementing an API with FastAPI

To begin, you'll implement your API. There are two main components here that you need to implement. The first is called your *web framework*. The web framework is responsible for the actual application logic of your API. It is what you will use to define what should happen when a user makes a request to a URL on your server. The different URL paths that a user might access are called *routes*, and using your web framework, you can define the appropriate response for each route. For example, if a user queries the route /question, you might want to implement some logic that responds with an answer.

The following code shows an example implementation of what your routes should look like. This code uses FastAPI, one of the most popular Python web frameworks, but it is very similar to other popular frameworks like Flask.

```
import json
from abc import ABC, abstractmethod
from typing_extensions import Annotated
```

```python
from pydantic import BaseModel
from pydantic_settings import BaseSettings,
SettingsConfigDict
from fastapi import Depends, FastAPI
from openai import OpenAI

from app.framework import (
    EquationPipeline,
    PromptNode,
    init_client
)
from app.config import get_settings

app = FastAPI()
settings = get_settings()
client, get_completion = init_client(settings
.OPENAI_API_KEY)

# Model for incoming requests
class MathRequest(BaseModel):
    equation: str
    with_cot: bool

@app.post('/equation')
async def equation(request: MathRequest):
    pipeline = EquationPipeline(generate=get_
completion, with_cot=request.with_cot)
    output = pipeline.run(prompt=request.equation)
    return output
```

You may notice that there are several references in this code to
utility files like `app.config`. These were included for the sake of
brevity, but if you'd like to see the full code, you can visit this book's
GitHub repository.

The actual routing logic here is very simple. When a user hits the /equation route, the app will run the EquationPipeline and return a response. For example, submitting the following JSON request via CURL:

```
{
  "equation": "8^6 - 4 * 6",
  "with_cot": true
}
```

returns the following:

```
8^6 means 8 multiplied by itself 6 times. So, 8^6 =
8 * 8 * 8 * 8 * 8 * 8 = 262,144. Now, we can
substitute this value into the equation: 262,144 -
4 * 6. Multiplying 4 by 6 gives us 24, so the equation
becomes 262,144 - 24. Finally, we can solve this by
subtracting 24 from 262,144, giving us a final answer
of 262,120. Therefore, the solution to the equation
is 262,120.
```

But you can't actually access your routes yet, and this is because your FastAPI application is not yet running on a server. For this, you'll need a web server, and the most popular option to pair with FastAPI is Uvicorn.

Implementing Uvicorn

Uvicorn is an asynchronous server gateway interface (ASGI) web server built for Python. This mouthful basically means it is capable of handling asynchronous requests. Using it is pretty straightforward, though you are invited to dive deeper into the documentation. Simply run this:

```
pip install "uvicorn[standard]"
```

Then, from the directory containing your application module, run the following:

```
uvicorn main:app -reload
```

Now, a Uvicorn application should be running, hosting your FastAPI application, and reloading anytime you change a file.

And *voila*! You have a basic user-facing API.

Monitoring an LLM

When deploying an LLM, you need to monitor most of what you'd normally track for a machine learning model, with some additional requirements. You want to track things like usage, as the more tokens you use, the more expensive your inference becomes. You also may want to track sequences of inferences (often referred to as *chains*), depending on your use case. Finally, you may also want to collect user feedback on your inferences, which will need to be logged and correctly associated with the right inference chain.

To implement this kind of tracking, you will be using Comet LLM, the opensource LLM tracking library from Comet. As in our previous examples, we've deliberately chosen a library whose API is simple and similar to other popular choices, such that switching will not be difficult should you choose to use different tools.

In your projects .env file, which is where you should store secrets like your API keys, you will need to add the following lines:

```
COMET_API_KEY='[YOUR_COMET_API_KEY]'
COMET_WORKSPACE='[YOUR_COMET_USERNAME]'
COMET_PROJECT_NAME=llmops-project
```

Putting Together an Application

Once that is done, you can run `pip install comet-llm` and update your `get_completion()` function with the following code (if you're following along from the repository, `get_completion()` is defined in the `framework.py` file):

```python
def get_completion(
    prompt,
    model="gpt-3.5-turbo-instruct",
    temperature=0,
    max_tokens=2000,
    **kwargs
):
    response = client.completions.create(
        model=model,
        prompt=prompt,
        temperature=temperature,
        max_tokens=max_tokens,
        **kwargs
    )

    comet_llm.log_prompt(
        prompt=prompt,
        output=response.choices[0].text,
        metadata= {
            "usage.prompt_tokens": response
.choices[0].usage.prompt_tokens,
            "usage.completion_tokens": response
.choices[0].usage.completion_tokens,
            "usage.total_tokens": response
.choices[0].usage.total_tokens,
            "temperature": temperature,
            "max_tokens": max_tokens,
```

```
        "model": model
    },

)


return response.choices[0].text
```

Now, when you query your API, all the relevant data will be logged in Comet, where you can analyze and dissect later.

Dockerizing Your Service

The final step in preparing a service for production is to wrap it in a container. For this example, you will be using Docker and DockerHub.

A *container* is a lightweight, stand-alone package that encapsulates a piece of software, making it possible to run uniformly and consistently across different computing environments. Unlike traditional virtual machines, containers do not bundle an entire operating system; instead, they include only the application and its dependencies, libraries, and other necessary binaries. This approach ensures that the software runs the same way, regardless of where the container is deployed, thus solving the common issue of "it works on my machine."

In MLOps, containers are especially important, as they provide a way for data scientists to encapsulate the exact environment needed for a model. This way, it is not left to an operations team to try to reimplement a model for production. Models are therefore much more reproducible.

One of the many benefits of wrapping your service in a container is that it is easy to deploy. You can run the service locally or on any cloud provider you'd like, all without modifying your container. This also makes it easier to scale, as you can simply replicate your container.

The template for your container is called an *image*, and the most popular platform for creating and managing your containers and images is Docker. You can easily install Docker via their official site.

Once installed, you can begin containerizing your service. First you'll need to create a file in your project's root directory called `Dockerfile`. This is where you will input the raw instructions for your image. Your Dockerfile should look like this:

```
# Use an official Python runtime as a parent image
FROM python:3.10-slim

# Set the working directory in the container
WORKDIR /usr/src/app

# Copy the current directory contents into the
container at /usr/src/app
COPY . .

# Install any needed packages specified in
requirements.txt
RUN pip install --no-cache-dir -r requirements.txt

# Make port 8000 available to the world outside
this container
EXPOSE 8000

# Define environment variable
ENV PYTHONUNBUFFERED=1
```

```
# Run app.py when the container launches
CMD ["uvicorn", "app.main:app", "--host", "0.0.0.0",
"--port", "8000"]
```

In this file, you've installed your requirements, set up your server, exposed the port users will be accessing, and run your Uvicorn server.

Remember, if you want more context for any of this code, you can see the entire codebase at this book's GitHub repo.

Once you have a Dockerfile, you need to create a template for Docker Compose. Docker Compose is a service that gives you more control over your container, allowing you to specify resources and more. To use Docker Compose, you simply create a file called docker-compose.yml that looks like this:

```
version: '3.8'

services:
 api:
   build: .
   command: uvicorn app.main:app --host 0.0.0.0
--port 8000
   volumes:
     - .:/usr/src/app
   ports:
     - "8000:8000"
   env_file:
     - .env
```

This file defines a service called api and tells Docker where its most important files are (like the .env file), along with other key information, like the command to run and ports to open.

Once you have these all built, you can run docker compose up from your terminal and your app should immediately start up.

Deploying Your Own LLM

Now, what if you don't want to use the OpenAI models? Fortunately, you can deploy almost any other LLM as a stand-alone service without any major changes to your existing user-facing API.

The reason is that many popular LLM serving solutions, like the one you'll be using here, have intentionally built their APIs to be compatible with the OpenAI libraries. So, all you have to do is update the URL used by the OpenAI library to point at your deployed model, and everything will work the same.

To start, you need to deploy a model. To make this easy, you'll be using three popular tools:

- **vLLM:** An open-source library for serving LLMs. It implements various forms of quantization and inference optimizations out of the box, giving you high-throughput inference without any of the extra infrastructure work.

- **SkyPilot:** An open-source framework that allows you to run vLLM on any cloud provider.

- **Hugging Face:** The most popular platform in the world of language models, providing free hosting of models, along with super popular libraries like *Transformers*.

Your first task is simply to build an API server using vLLM. First, you need to download vLLM via `pip install vllm`. After doing so, you can deploy an OpenAI API compatible server by running the following code from the command line:

```
$ python -m vllm.entrypoints.openai.api_server \
$ --model facebook/opt-125m
```

The amount of work vLLM is doing under the hood here is really impressive. It fetches the `facebook/opt-125m` model from Hugging Face and automatically implements a heap of optimizations specifically for that model. It implements *Paged Attention*, which is essentially a more efficient form of self-attention for Transformer models. It also uses an optimized CUDA kernel, performs various optimizations on the model itself, and can support many kinds of quantization automatically. Compute Unified Device Architecture (CUDA) is a platform for parallel computing, created by NVIDIA.

From your side, however, it is simply another API that you can ping. For example, you can run inference simply by pinging the API like so:

```
curl http://localhost:8000/v1/completions \
    -H "Content-Type: application/json" \
    -d '{
        "model": "facebook/opt-125m",
        "prompt": "San Francisco is a",
        "max_tokens": 7,
        "temperature": 0
    }'
```

Now, the next question is how do you deploy vLLM to the cloud? That's where SkyPilot comes in. First, you need to install SkyPilot with the following:

```
$ pip install "skypilot-nightly[aws,gcp,azure,oci,
lambda,runpod,ibm,scp,kubernetes]"  # choose your
clouds
```

Once installed, you can begin defining your deployment. Like many DevOps tools, SkyPilot uses a YAML template file to customize deployments. In your project directory, create a file titled `service.yaml` and populate it with the following code:

```yaml
# service.yaml
name: flan-t5-large

service:
  readiness_probe: /v1/models
  replicas: 2


# Fields below describe each replica.
resources:
  cloud: aws
  ports: 8080
  accelerators: t4

setup: |
  conda create -n vllm python=3.9 -y
  conda activate vllm
  pip install vllm

run: |
  conda activate vllm
  python -m vllm.entrypoints.openai.api_server \
    --tensor-parallel-size $SKYPILOT_NUM_GPUS_PER_NODE \
    --host 0.0.0.0 --port 8080 \
    --model google/flan-t5-large
```

If you're unfamiliar with YAML templates or DevOps generally, the previous might be a bit confusing, but it's actually very straightforward. The `service` block defines the high-level configuration for your service. In this case, you're instructing the system as to which cloud it should use, where it should ping to see if the service is ready, and how many *replicas* should be launched. A replica is simply a copy of your service. You'll often have several deployed, in the event that one is at capacity. Every other block in the YAML specifies something about each replica. For example, the `resources` block specifies which ports to open and what kind of GPUs are needed. The `setup` block defines the commands to run on initial launch, and the `run` block specifies what to run when everything is ready.

You can get much more complex with your configuration if you'd like. You can use spot instances, for example, unused instances that public clouds offer at a discount, or configure the precise behavior by which your service should autoscale additional replicas. You're encouraged to explore the SkyPilot documentation if this interests you.

Once your YAML is filled out, all you have to do is run `sky serve up service.yaml`. Depending on your local setup, you may be prompted for your cloud authorization keys. Once your YAML is processed, you should see an interface like this:

```
Service from YAML spec: service.yaml
Service Spec:
Readiness probe method:          GET /v1/models
Readiness initial delay seconds: 1200
Replica autoscaling policy:      Fixed 2 replicas
Each replica will use the following resources
(estimated):
AWS: Fetching availability zones mapping...I 02-01
15:40:11 optimizer.py:694] == Optimizer ==
I 02-01 15:40:11 optimizer.py:705] Target:
minimizing cost
I 02-01 15:40:11 optimizer.py:717] Estimated cost:
$0.5 / hour
I 02-01 15:40:11 optimizer.py:717]
```

Putting Together an Application

```
I 02-01 15:40:11 optimizer.py:840] Considered
resources (1 node):
I 02-01 15:40:11 optimizer.py:910] ------------------
-----------------------------------------------------
-----------------
I 02-01 15:40:11 optimizer.py:910]  CLOUD    INSTANCE
vCPUs   Mem(GB)   ACCELERATORS   REGION/ZONE   COST
($)   CHOSEN
I 02-01 15:40:11 optimizer.py:910] ------------------
-----------------------------------------------------
-----------------
I 02-01 15:40:11 optimizer.py:910]  AWS     g4dn
.xlarge   4       16       T4:1            us-east-1
0.53                              ✔
I 02-01 15:40:11 optimizer.py:910] ------------------
-----------------------------------------------------
-----------------
I 02-01 15:40:11 optimizer.py:910]
I 02-01 15:40:11 optimizer.py:928] Multiple AWS
instances satisfy T4:1. The cheapest AWS(g4dn.xlarge,
{'T4': 1}, ports=['8080']) is considered among:
I 02-01 15:40:11 optimizer.py:928] ['g4dn.xlarge',
'g4dn.2xlarge', 'g4dn.4xlarge', 'g4dn.8xlarge',
'g4dn.16xlarge'].
I 02-01 15:40:11 optimizer.py:928]
I 02-01 15:40:11 optimizer.py:934] To list more
details, run 'sky show-gpus T4'.
Launching a new service 'sky-service-a6ea'.
Proceed? [Y/n]: n
```

After responding Y, your model service will be spun up! You have a deployed model. You can see the endpoint of the model by running sky serve status, which will return a table as shown in Figure 5.7.

Machine Learning Upgrade

```
[(sky-serve) → ~ sky serve status
Services
NAME   UPTIME  STATUS  REPLICAS  ENDPOINT
vllm   7m 43s  READY   2/2       3.84.15.251:30001

Service Replicas
SERVICE_NAME  ID  IP            LAUNCHED      RESOURCES           STATUS  REGION
vllm          1   34.66.255.4   11 mins ago   1x GCP({'L4': 8}))  READY   us-central1
vllm          2   35.221.37.64  15 mins ago   1x GCP({'L4': 8}))  READY   us-east4
```

Figure 5.7 Deployed model

This endpoint can be used in exactly the same way you'd use the OpenAI API. In fact, you can actually pass in this endpoint as the base URL to your OpenAI client, as demonstrated here:

```
client = OpenAI(base_url="YOUR-URL")
```

You can specify any model you'd like to serve from Hugging Face simply by specifying it in your YAML. This means that if you'd like to deploy a custom model you've trained, all you need to do is upload it to Hugging Face and point your service at it.

And now, you have a fully functioning service!

Wrapping Things Up

We've covered a lot of ground in building applications using various technologies. From prototyping with Gradio to creating graphics with Plotnine and deploying models as APIs, we've explored different aspects of application development.

You've learned how to implement APIs using Fast API and Uvicorn and the importance of monitoring for optimal performance. Dockerization has shown us how to streamline deployment processes, providing us with more easily achievable flexibility and scalability.

There is a lot to digest in this chapter, and you shouldn't feel bad if you struggle with any of the material. Inference and deployment are expansive, ever-changing fields, and as you continue to build your own production systems, you can refer to this chapter or the GitHub for the book as needed.

Rounding Out the ML Life Cycle

You've learned a bit about monitoring and productionizing models so far in this book, but in this chapter, you're going to go a step deeper. Monitoring is one of the most essential components of a production machine learning (ML) system but is the most overlooked. Partially, this is because monitoring is not as prominent in research settings. As a result, monitoring is often treated as a strictly engineering problem.

In this chapter, you'll explore monitoring from a different lens. You'll conceptualize monitoring as part of your model's life cycle, applying a data scientist's mindset to use monitoring as a tool for experimentation, evaluation, and retraining.

Note that we're not going to dive too deeply into some topics around model serving, which generally fall to a platform engineer. For example, projects like Nvidia Triton are fantastic for serving models with optimal latency and performance, but implementing them is largely a software engineering project and one that will be highly platform dependent.

Before you can monitor a model, you must, of course, take it into production.

Deploying a Simple Random Forest Model

We've focused quite a bit on large language models (LLMs) so far in this book. In the following sections, you'll again be working with

LLMs, but initially, you'll be building with a more traditional machine learning model. In particular, you'll learn how to implement basic monitoring for a random forest regression model.

To move things along quickly, you'll train a random forest regressor using scikit-learn (shown in Listing 6.1) and perhaps one of the most ubiquitous datasets in machine learning, the California housing price dataset.

Listing 6.1   Random Forest Regressor for California Housing Price Dataset

```
import comet_ml
import pandas as pd

comet_ml.init(api_key="YOUR-COMET-API-KEY)

# Fetch artifact containing your dataset
experiment = comet_ml.Experiment()
housing_data_artifact = experiment.get_artifact
('ckaiser/housing-data-baseline')
housing_data_artifact.download('./datasets')

# Load data into a Dataframe
housing_data = pd.read_csv('./datasets/housing-
data.csv')

# Import scikit libraries for training
from sklearn.model_selection import train_test_split
from sklearn.ensemble import RandomForestRegressor
from sklearn.metrics import mean_squared_error

# Initialize training parameters
params = {
```

```
        "n_estimators": 1000,
        "max_depth": 6,
        "min_samples_split": 5,
        "warm_start":True,
        "oob_score":True,
        "random_state": 42,
}

# Split train and test datasets
train, test = train_test_split(
        housing_data, test_size=0.15, random_state=params
['random_state']
)

y_train = train['target']
x_train = train.drop(columns=['target'])

y_test = test['target']
x_test = test.drop(columns=['target'])

# Fit the model on the training data
model = RandomForestRegressor(**params)
model.fit(x_train, y_train)

# Predict on the test set
y_test_pred = model.predict(x_test)

# Evaluate the model
accuracy = mean_squared_error(y_test, y_test_pred)
print(f'Validation Accuracy: {accuracy}')

# Pickle and save model
import pickle
```

```
with open('./baseline.pkl', 'wb') as f:
    pickle.dump(model, f)

# Version and store model via Comet Artifacts
model_artifact = comet_ml.Artifact('baseline-
housing-model')
model_artifact.add('./baseline.pkl')
experiment.log_artifact(model_artifact)
```

Once the random forest regressor is trained, you need to serve
the model. You've read about model deployment in more detail in
previous chapters, so in this exercise, we'll keep things simple with
a straightforward FastAPI server you can run locally.

For the code exercises in the rest of this chapter, you'll need to
clone the Chapter-6 code of this book's GitHub repository. You
will be using some utility scripts contained inside the repository
throughout the following code samples, which have been omitted
from the text of this book for the sake of brevity. Once you've cloned
Chapter 6 from the repository, run the following bash commands
on Mac (or use PowerShell in Windows) from the root of the project to install all the necessary dependencies and to traverse to the
Chapter-6 code.

A *utility script* refers to a small program or script designed to perform specific tasks or provide commonly used functionalities that
are not part of the main functionality of an application. These
scripts are often created to streamline development workflows,
automate repetitive tasks, or provide auxiliary functions that can
be reused across multiple projects.

Machine Learning Upgrade

Let's start in on the code.

```
$ pip install -r requirements.txt
$ cd Chapter-6
```

In Listing 6.2, you'll initialize a FastAPI server, load your model, and establish a /prediction route for serving model inferences.

Listing 6.2   Serving a Model with FastAPI

```
from fastapi import Depends, FastAPI
import httpx
import pickle  # For loading the scikit-learn model
import comet_ml

from functools import lru_cache
from typing_extensions import Annotated

from . import config

app = FastAPI()
model = None  # Placeholder for the loaded model

# See earlier chapters for guidance around defining
environment variables
@lru_cache
def get_settings():
    return config.Settings()

@app.on_event("startup")
async def startup_event(settings: Annotated[config
.Settings, Depends(get_settings)]):
    global model
```

```
comet_ml.init(api_key=settings.comet_api_key)
experiment = comet_ml.APIExperiment()
model_artifact = experiment.get_artifact
('baseline-housing-model')
model_artifact.download('./')
with open('./baseline.pkl', 'rb') as f:
    model = pickle.load(f)

from fastapi import HTTPException
from pydantic import BaseModel
import numpy as np

class PredictionInput(BaseModel):
    features: list  # Assuming a simple list
of features

@app.post("/prediction/")
async def make_prediction(input_data: PredictionInput):
    try:
        prediction = model.predict([input_data
.features])
        return {"prediction": prediction.tolist()}
# Convert numpy array to list
    except Exception as e:
        raise HTTPException(status_code=400,
detail=str(e))
```

There are better ways to persist a model than .pkl files, but for the sake of this project, there is no need to overcomplicate things. With a model deployed, you can now begin implementing some basic monitoring.

An Introduction to Model Monitoring

Monitoring is a somewhat ambiguous term in machine learning. *Explainability, interpretability*, and *monitoring* all tend to get lumped together in conversation. For the sake of this project, *model monitoring* refers to tracking our models and our data to identify deviations from their baseline metrics. Everything you implement in your monitoring setup is in service of answering a simple question: has your model's performance changed, and why?

With that out of the way, let's dig into a simple implementation. The first decision to make in building your monitoring system is around logging. Later, you will define metrics and build dashboards for analyzing the data generated by your model, but before you can do that, you must decide how you will be collecting that data.

One of the bigger decisions here has to do with how real time your monitoring needs to be. If you're operating a certain level of scale or if you have a very complex system that involves rapid redeployments, you may need truly real-time model monitoring, in which data is being constantly streamed from your model as it performs. In most situations, however, you will be able to log your data and collect analytics asynchronously. This is especially true when you are first engineering your system and just need something that works.

To start, you'll focus solely on logging your data. The simplest way to do this is to use a background task, which executes after a successful request is returned by FastAPI.

```
from fastapi import HTTPException, BackgroundTasks
from pydantic import BaseModel
import numpy as np
from csv import DictWriter
```

```
async def log_data(data: dict):
    with open('./production_data.csv', "a+") as f:
        d = DictWriter(f, fieldnames=list
(data.keys()))
        d.writerow(data)

class PredictionInput(BaseModel):
    features: list  # Assuming a simple list
of features

@app.post("/prediction/")
async def make_prediction(background_tasks:
BackgroundTasks, input_data: PredictionInput):
    try:
        prediction = model.predict([input_data
.features])
        result = {"prediction": prediction.tolist()}
# Convert numpy array to list
        logged_data =  input_data.dict()
        logged_data['prediction'] = result
['prediction']
        # Add the log_data function to background
tasks
        background_tasks.add_task(log_data, data=
logged_data)

    except Exception as e:
        raise HTTPException(status_code=400,
detail=str(e))
```

With your data logged, you can now move on to calculating metrics. One of the core challenges of monitoring models is collecting outcome data. That is, if users don't share any data with you about the accuracy of your predictions, it's hard to use their data to assess your model. Collecting this outcome data is very context dependent. With some projects, like recommendation engines, you'll be able to collect data directly from user behavior. In others, you may ask for user feedback. In this example, you would likely collect data asynchronously at a later date (for example, you may find new housing data to tell you the price of houses that fit the user's input). For this project, we'll pretend you've performed this post-hoc augmentation and now have a dataset for evaluating and potentially retraining your model.

Now, you can calculate some metrics.

Metric Categories

When discussing model monitoring, metrics are often placed in three distinct categories.

- **Performance metrics:** These are metrics specifically concerned with the performance of your model on its given task. Traditionally, it includes metrics such as accuracy, precision, and recall.

- **System metrics:** These are the sort of metrics a platform team might be particularly interested in, such as resource utilization, throughput, latency, etc. You can loosely define system metrics as anything related to the performance of the underlying infrastructure.

- **Business metrics:** These are metrics connected to particular business outcomes. For example, a sales forecasting model might have a performance metric of "accuracy" but might still be connected to business key performance indicators (KPIs).

In this chapter, you'll be focused on performance metrics.

First, load in the dataset of user-submitted data.

```python
# Load new dataset of user data, which you've
asyncronously updated
import requests

with requests.get('NEW DATASET') as r:
    with open('new_dataset.csv', 'w+') as f:
        f.write(r.text)

import pandas as pd
dataset = pd.read_csv('./new_dataset.csv')

# Load historic dataset

# Comet Artifact

reference_dataset = pd.read_csv(old_dataset)
```

Now, you can define your metrics. Later, you'll use a fantastic open-source library for monitoring, but initially, you'll implement a simple system from scratch in Python. To start, you're going to define a Report class. This class will serve as a central location for your metrics pipeline, your datasets, and your display functions. Within an initialized Report instance, you will establish your reference dataset as well as the metrics you'll be calculating.

```python
class Report:
    def __init__(self, baseline, metrics=[]):
        self.super
        self.metrics = metrics
        self.statistics = {}
        self.baseline = baseline
```

```
def run(self, dataset):
    for metric in self.metrics:
        self.statistics[metric.name] = metric.run
(self.baseline, dataset)

    print("Report is ready!")
```

Next, you should define a `Metric` class.

```
class Metric:
    def __init__(self, name, *args, **kwargs):
        self.name = name
        self.metric_kwargs = kwargs

    def run(self, baseline, data):
        pass
```

Now, define a single metric to get started. A good metric for calculating drift here would be something typical in a data scientist's toolkit, like the population stability index (PSI). Listing 6.3 shows the implementation of PSI as a metric using the `Metric` class.

Listing 6.3 Implementing PSI as a Metric

```
class PSI(Metric):
    def __init__(self, bucket_types='bins',
buckets=10, axis=0):
        super().__init__()
        self.name = 'PSI'
        self.bucket_types = bucket_types
        self.buckets = buckets
        self.axis = axis

    def _calculate_psi(self, expected, actual):
        """
```

171

```
        Calculate the PSI (population stability index)
across all variables
        """
        bucket_type = self.bucket_type
        buckets = self.buckets
        axis = self.axis

        def psi(expected_array, actual_array, buckets):
            def scale_range (input, min, max):
                input += -(np.min(input))
                input /= np.max(input) / (max - min)
                input += min
                return input

            breakpoints = np.arange(0, buckets + 1) /
(buckets) * 100
            if bucket_type == 'bins':
                breakpoints = scale_range(breakpoints,
np.min(expected_array), np.max(expected_array))
            elif bucket_type == 'quantiles':
                breakpoints = np.percentile(expected_
array, breakpoints)

            expected_percents = np.histogram(expected_
array, breakpoints)[0] / len(expected_array)
            actual_percents = np.histogram(actual_
array, breakpoints)[0] / len(actual_array)

            def sub_psi(e_perc, a_perc):
                """Calculate the actual PSI value from
comparing the expected and actual distributions."""
                if a_perc == 0:
                    return 0
```

```
                    elif e_perc == 0:
                        return a_perc * np.log(a_perc /
0.01)
                    else:
                        return (e_perc - a_perc) * np.log
(e_perc / a_perc)

                psi_value = np.sum(sub_psi(expected_
percents[i], actual_percents[i]) for i in range
(0, len(expected_percents)))
                return psi_value

        psi_values = pd.Series(index=expected.columns)
        for col in expected.columns:
            psi_values[col] = psi(expected[col],
actual[col], buckets=buckets, bucket_type=bucket_type)

        return psi_values

    def run(self, baseline, data):
        output = self._calculate_psi(baseline, data)
        return output
```

Now, you can initialize a new report utilizing your new metric.

```
PSIDrift = PSI("PSI")
DriftReport = Report(reference_dataset, [PSIDrift])
```

And run your report.

```
DriftReport.run(current_dataset)
DriftReport.statistics
```

Model Drift vs. Data Drift

Drift is typically discussed in two contexts: model drift and data drift. While related, the two are distinct. *Model drift*, or concept drift, refers to the scenario where the statistical properties of the target variable, which the model is trying to predict, changes over time. This drift means that the patterns or relationships that the model learned during training no longer hold, leading to a degradation in model performance.

Data drift, on the other hand, pertains to changes in the distribution or properties of the input data fed into the model. Unlike model drift, where the focus is on the target variable, data drift focuses on the predictors or features. Changes in purchasing habits in a recommendation model, for example, is a common cause of data drift. Detecting data drift involves statistical tests to compare the distribution of data at different points in time.

Addressing both forms of drift requires frequent evaluation and monitoring of models and datasets.

This is just a basic example. You're encouraged to experiment with different metrics and displays. However, even this simple example is deceptively powerful. The pipeline has the following features:

- Datasets are tracked and version-controlled via Comet Artifacts.
- Metrics are calculated in a consistent, transparent fashion with your report.
- Everything is reproducible due to your thorough tracking and versioning.

There is still plenty to implement—scheduling runs of your report, storing the output statistics somewhere accessible, and so forth. But even a setup this basic can take you far.

Model Monitoring with Evidently AI

In actual production situations, you're not going to be building your own monitoring library. At least, not typically. In most cases, you'll use an existing solution. One of the best platforms for monitoring currently is Evidently, an open-source monitoring and analytics library from Evidently AI. As you explore Evidently in the following examples, you'll notice that the API design is very similar to what you've implemented so far.

To familiarize you with the library briefly, Evidently uses a centralized `Report` class, similar to the class you implemented earlier. This report accepts an array of Metric instances, which similarly are run when you call `Report.run()` on your datasets. Here's an example:

```
from evidently.report import Report
from evidently.metric_preset import DataDriftPreset

report = Report(metrics=[
    DataDriftPreset(),
])
```

One of the many nice aspects of Evidently is that it implements many different metrics out of the box with its `metric_preset` module. Here's an example:

```
from evidently.metrics import ColumnSummaryMetric,
ColumnQuantileMetric, ColumnDriftMetric

report = Report(metrics=[
    ColumnSummaryMetric(column_name='AveRooms'),
```

```
    ColumnQuantileMetric(column_name='AveRooms',
quantile=0.25),
    ColumnDriftMetric(column_name='AveRooms')
])

report.run(reference_data=reference, current_
data=current)
```

Additionally, Evidently gives you nice visualizations automatically. Simply display the `report` object in your notebook, and you will see the chart shown in Figure 6.1.

Take some time to explore the automatic dashboarding functionality in Evidently. You can see more in-depth analytics on individual features and customize the dashboards to your liking.

This is all very powerful, but your ultimate goal is to turn these disparate components into an automated pipeline. That's what you'll be setting up next, and you'll be doing it using a large language model.

Building a Model Monitoring System

In this project, you'll build an end-to-end pipeline for model monitoring, and you'll also make use of a pretrained LLM. The code you'll write will allow you to use an OpenAI model like GPT-4 or a model deployed on vLLM (which you learned to do in Chapter 5).

To start, define a new FastAPI server with two routes, a `/prediction` route for serving inference and a `/feedback` route for collecting user feedback on the responses, as shown in Listing 6.4. The API you'll be building is specifically focused on question-answering. You can reuse the startup sections of the API you wrote previously. Mostly, you'll be updating your routes.

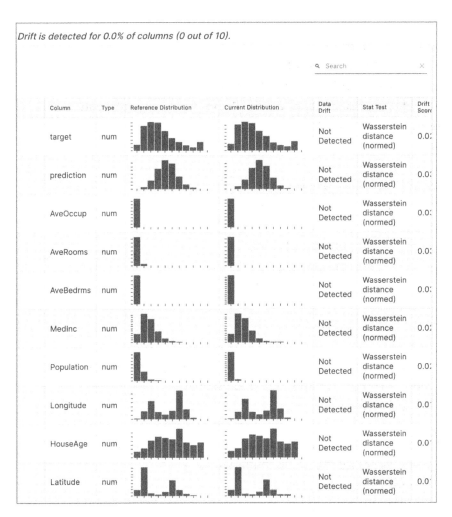

Drift is detected for 0.0% of columns (0 out of 10).

Column	Type	Reference Distribution	Current Distribution	Data Drift	Stat Test	Drift Score
target	num			Not Detected	Wasserstein distance (normed)	0.0:
prediction	num			Not Detected	Wasserstein distance (normed)	0.0:
AveOccup	num			Not Detected	Wasserstein distance (normed)	0.0:
AveRooms	num			Not Detected	Wasserstein distance (normed)	0.0:
AveBedrms	num			Not Detected	Wasserstein distance (normed)	0.0:
MedInc	num			Not Detected	Wasserstein distance (normed)	0.0:
Population	num			Not Detected	Wasserstein distance (normed)	0.0:
Longitude	num			Not Detected	Wasserstein distance (normed)	0.0
HouseAge	num			Not Detected	Wasserstein distance (normed)	0.0
Latitude	num			Not Detected	Wasserstein distance (normed)	0.0

Figure 6.1 Model monitoring

Listing 6.4   Defining Prediction and Feedback Routes

```
import comet_llm
from comet_llm.query_dsl import TraceMetadata
from fastapi import HTTPException
from pydantic import BaseModel
from uuid import uuid4
from openai import OpenAI
```

```
client = OpenAI (
    api_key="YOUR-API-KEY",
    # base_url="YOUR-API-URL"
    # Uncomment the above line to use your own model
deployed with vLLM
)

async def log_prompt(data: dict):
    comet_llm.log_prompt(
        prompt=data['prompt'],
        output=data['output'],
        metadata={
            'id': data['id']
        }
    )


# Define the request model for the prediction route
class PredictionRequest(BaseModel):
    question: str


# Define the request model for the feedback route
class FeedbackRequest(BaseModel):
    conversation_id: str
    score: float


@app.post("/prediction/")
async def prediction(background_tasks:
BackgroundTasks, request: PredictionRequest):
    try:
        # Generate a unique identifier for the
conversation
        conversation_id = str(uuid4 ())
        completion = client.chat.completions.create (
```

```
            model="gpt-4",
            messages=[{"role": "user", "content":
request.question}],
        )
        answer = completion.choices[0].message.content
        log = {
            "prompt": request.question,
            "output": answer,
            "id": conversation_id
        }
        response = {"answer": answer, "conversation_
id": conversation_id}
        background_tasks.add_task(log_prompt,
data=log)
        return response
    except Exception as e:
        raise HTTPException (status_code=400,
detail=str(e))


@app.post("/feedback")
async def feedback(background_tasks: BackgroundTasks,
request: FeedbackRequest):
    try:
        api = comet_llm.API()
        # An LLMTrace is the object Comet uses to
represent the query/response
        trace = api.query(
            workspace="YOUR-WORKSPACE",
            project_name="YOUR-PROJECT",
            query=(TraceMetadata("id") == request
.conversation_id)
        )
```

```
        trace.log_user_feedback(request.score)

        return {"status": "Success"}

    except Exception as e:
        raise HTTPException(status_code=400,
detail=str(e))
```

Notice that Listing 6.4 uses Comet LLM, the open-source prompt management framework we touched on in Chapter 5, for logging prompts and responses.

Next, you need to write a script to convert your logged data into a version-controlled Artifact, as shown in Listing 6.5.

Listing 6.5 Script to Convert Logged Data

```
import comet_llm
from comet_llm.query_dsl import TraceMetadata,
Duration, Timestamp, UserFeedback
import json

def llm_data_to_artifact(start_time, end_time,
artifact_name):
    comet_llm.init()
    api = comet_llm.API()
    traces = api.query(
        workspace="YOUR-WORKSPACE",
        project_name="YOUR-PROJECT",
        query=((Timestamp() > start_time) &
(Timestamp() < end_time))
    )

    json_blob = []
```

```python
    # api.query() returns a list of LLMTraces that
match our query parameter
    for trace in traces:
        trace_data = trace._get_trace_data()
        data = {
            "inputs": trace_data['chain_inputs'],
            "outputs": trace_data['chain_outputs'],
            "metadata": trace_data['metadata']
        }
        json_blob.append(data)

    file_name = f"{start_time}-{end_time}.json"

    with open(file_name, 'w+') as  f:
        json.dump(json_blob, f)

    experiment = comet_ml.Experiment()

    # Try to access existing artifact, if we've
previously created one
    try:
        artifact = experiment.get_artifact
(artifact_name)
    except:
        artifact = comet_ml.Artifact(artifact_name)

    artifact.add(file_name)
    experiment.log_artifact(artifact)
```

Now, you want to use this data in your Evidently reporting. Before you do any pipeline work, you'll need to create an Evidently project (you'll have to register for a free account to use Evidently's Cloud API).

```
from evidently.ui.workspace.cloud import
CloudWorkspace

ws = CloudWorkspace(
    token="YOUR_TOKEN_HERE",
    url="https://app.evidently.cloud"
)


project = ws.create_project("Housing Data Monitoring")
project.description = "A first project with Evidently"
project.save()
```

Your pipeline needs to move this data into an Evidently report.
To achieve this, you can use the following function, which will access
a reference dataset and a single batch of production data from a single Artifact:

```
from evidently.report import Report
from evidently.metrics import DatasetSummaryMetric
from evidently.metric_preset import DataDriftPreset

# Assumes you've uploaded a reference dataset as
# a json file
def run_reports(artifact_name, batch_filename,
reference_filename="reference.json", report_name=
"data_drift_report.json"):
    ws = CloudWorkspace(
        token="YOUR_TOKEN_HERE",
        url="https://app.evidently.cloud"
    )
```

```
# Update with your project id
project = ws.get_project("PROJECT_ID")


experiment = comet_ml.Experiment()
artifact = experiment.get_artifact(artifact_name)
# Creates a ./tmp directory for asset downloads
artifact.download('./tmp')
reference_data = json.load(f"./tmp/{reference_
filename}")
    batch_data = json.load(f"./tmp/{batch_filename}")
    data_summary_report = Report(metrics=[
        DatasetSummaryMetric (),
    ])

    data_summary_report.run(reference_data=reference_
data, current_data=batch_data)
    data_summary_report.save_json(report_name)
    ws.add_report(project.id, data_summary_report)
```

Now, you need to schedule this script to run every 24 hours. In a production setting, you'd likely schedule this job using a product provided by your particular cloud, like AWS Batch, but for the sake of this project, you'll schedule the job to run on your local machine.

To start, write the following function at the bottom of your Python script, which you can title monitoring.py:

```
def parse_args():
    parser = argparse.ArgumentParser(description=
'Process command line arguments.')

    # Adding required arguments
    parser.add_argument('--reference_dataset',
type=str, required=False, help='Path to the reference
dataset', default="reference.json")
```

```
    parser.add_argument('--batch_filename', type=str,
required=True, help='Path to the batch file')
    parser.add_argument('--artifact_name', type=str,
required=True, help='Name of the artifact')
    parser.add_argument('--report_name', type=str,
required=False, help='Name of the report',
default="report.json")

    # Using custom type for datetime parsing
    def valid_date(s):
        try:
            return datetime.strptime(s, "%Y-%m-%d
%H:%M:%S")
        except ValueError:
            msg = "Not a valid date: '{0}'.".format(s)
            raise argparse.ArgumentTypeError(msg)

    parser.add_argument('--start_time', type=valid_
date, required=False, help="The Start Time in 'YYYY-
MM-DD HH:MM:SS' format", default=datetime.now()
- timedelta(days=1))
    parser.add_argument('--end_time', type=valid_date,
required=False, help="The End Time in 'YYYY-MM-DD
HH:MM:SS' format", default=datetime.now())

    args = parser.parse_args()
    return args

def main():
    args = parse_args()
    llm_data_to_artifact(args.artifact_name, args
.start_time, args.end_time)
```

```
    run_reports(args.artifact_name, args.batch_
filename, args.reference_filename, args.report_name)


if __name__ == "main":
    main()
```

Now, you want to schedule this script to run every 24 hours. On UNIX operating systems like Mac and Linux, you can do this using cron. First, run this:

```
crontab -e
```

This will open your crontab file in your default editor. This is the file where you input recurring tasks. Within this file, add the following line, updated to reflect your system:

```
0 0 * * * /usr/bin/python3 /home/user/scripts/
monitoring.py --reference_dataset "reference_dataset"
--artifact_name "dataset"
```

In Windows, you'll use the task scheduler, which will give you step-by-step instructions for scheduling a recurring task.

Take a moment to reflect on how much you've implemented here. With only a couple hundred lines of code, you've implemented a system that allows for the following:

- Users can query a large language model for question answering and record their feedback on the response.
- Your LLM behavior is fully tracked and recorded, with prompts, responses, and ratings all being saved.

- Your data is automatically version-controlled and used to construct new datasets in both Comet and Evidently.

- Your entire pipeline is run automatically with no manual input from you.

This is pretty great! Once everything is running, you can implement your dashboard however you like, following the process you learned earlier for building Evidently dashboards (see Figure 6.2).

You can get quite a bit out of Evidently's built-in metrics. You can analyze various features of your users' input text, including sentiment, word distribution, and topics. You can also see similar metrics collected from your model's responses. You can even see user feedback on your model's responses, in a format that allows you to investigate common threads in poorly performing responses. Finally, you're able to detect drift in your users' input as well as your model's output.

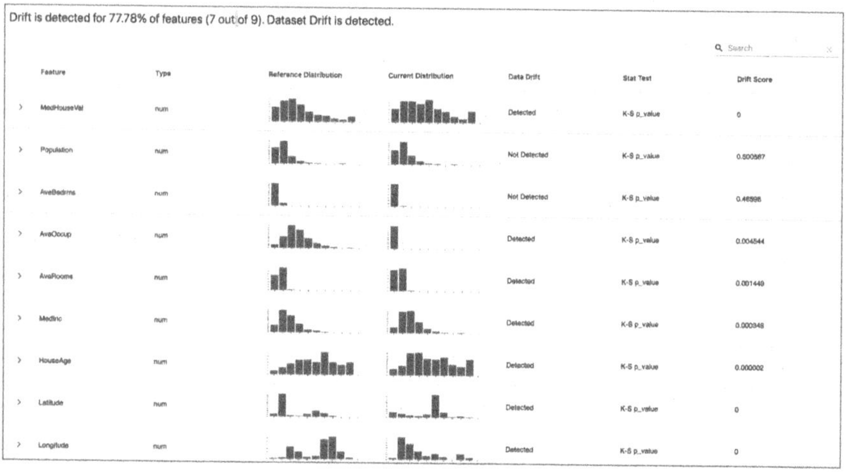

Figure 6.2 Evidently: Built-in metrics

From this, you have a complete snapshot of the health of your system at any given moment. You can use it simply to track the impact of different changes you make to your pipeline, to alert you when performance deteriorates, or even as the basis of a retraining pipeline. This system is easily adapted to any use case.

Final Thoughts on Monitoring

What you've built here can take you far in terms of monitoring. However, as you achieve new levels of scale and have greater demands for your monitoring, paying for a hosted third-party service becomes more advantageous. Some of the platforms you've used so far, like Comet, offer a paid production monitoring service, typically capable of real-time data collection, custom metrics, and incredibly high levels of scale.

The principles, however, will not change. Fundamentally, the ideas you've developed in these projects should carry you through on any monitoring project you decide to take on.

Review of Best Practices

This book was born by our desire to bridge traditional data science work in order to get to production systematically and reproducibly by focusing on the MLOps framework in a post-LLM world. The rapid changes in the size and scope of data projects has made MLOps—which has always been beneficial—now absolutely essential.

This chapter summarizes the framework covered in this book in four steps. After this recap, the rest of the chapter covers new trends and future potential developments in machine learning operations (MLOps) and large language models (LLMs).

Step 1: Understand the Problem

The first step involves defining the problem statement, ensuring data quality and implementing data governance. Arguably, these tasks are some of the most important pieces in ensuring the success of your project, and they have not changed with the advancements we've seen in the field or with the growth in popularity of LLMs.

- **Clarity of objectives:** Clearly define the problem objectives and get buy-in before developing the model. This has been the case for as long as analysts have been analyzing. Understanding the business goal ensures alignment between model outcomes and organizational needs, as you'll be less likely to end up with an abandoned project.

- **Data quality and preprocessing:** Invest significantly in data preprocessing, cleaning, and validation. As we discussed, the data is the most precious piece of your successful machine learning models. As time continues, the data is becoming more and more the differentiating factor in a business's market competitiveness and the impact your model will have, as it is much harder to replicate proprietary data than to use a similar algorithm.

- **Data governance:** Establish policies, processes, and standards to ensure the quality, integrity, security, and proper use of an organization's data. Effective data governance mitigates the risks of poor data quality, security breaches, and noncompliance. Organizations can proactively identify and address potential risks by implementing controls and monitoring mechanisms, protecting the company's reputation, and minimizing legal and financial exposure.

Step 2: Model Selection and Training

The second step involves the following tasks:

- **Model selection and experimentation:** Experiment with a model, or potentially multiple models, leveraging experiment tracking. Different models excel in various scenarios; experimentation helps identify the most suitable one. For LLMs, larger models generally have more parameters, allowing them to capture more complex patterns in data. However, larger models also require more computational resources for training and inference. Consider the trade-off between model size and resource requirements based on your available infrastructure. Evaluate the cost of using the language model, especially when it's offered through a cloud-based service. Consider the pricing structure and whether it aligns with your budget. Check whether the language model is actively being maintained.

- **Hyperparameter tuning and optimization:** If your use case requires fine-tuning on domain-specific data, check whether the language model supports fine-tuning. Not all models allow fine-tuning, and the process may have specific requirements and limitations. Systematic hyperparameter tuning techniques help to optimize the cross-validation score of your model. You would consider doing this to improve model performance, avoid overfitting or underfitting, enhance generalization, improve convergence and training speed, adapt to different datasets, or enhance robustness to noisy data. Some of the hyperparameter tuning techniques include the following:

  - *Grid search:* Grid search is the simplest algorithm for hyperparameter tuning and involves defining a hyperparameter grid and exhaustively evaluating all possible combinations. It systematically explores the hyperparameter space (an exhaustive search, going through all combinations), making it a reliable choice when the search space is relatively small and manageable.

  - *Random search:* Random search randomly samples hyperparameter combinations for model training and evaluation (not exhaustive). While it is more computationally efficient than grid search, it provides a good balance between exploration and exploitation, making it suitable for a broader range of hyperparameter spaces.

  - *Bayesian optimization:* Bayesian optimization leverages probabilistic models, keeping track of previous evaluation results, to predict the performance of hyperparameter combinations. Bayesian optimization is beneficial when the evaluation of hyperparameter sets is computationally expensive.

Additional levers you can use to optimize your model include adjusting the learning rate, batch size, or regularization techniques.

Warmup steps involve gradually increasing the learning rate during the initial training steps. This technique is specifically helpful for large language models, helping to stabilize training and improve convergence. It is commonly applied to prevent potential issues like exploding gradients at the beginning of training.

Batch size tuning involves experimenting with different batch sizes during training. The optimal batch size depends on the specific characteristics of the dataset and the available computational resources. Tuning batch size can impact the training speed and model generalization.

Regularization techniques, such as dropout rates and weight decay, are commonly used to prevent overfitting in both tabular data and large language models. Regularization helps control the complexity of the model, improving its generalization performance on unseen data.

Regularization refers to a category of techniques that attempt to help models generalize by decreasing the model's sensitivity to variance in the data. By doing this, the model is less likely to "overfit"—that is, learn the unique peculiarities of a given training dataset, peculiarities which do not generalize to the validation or test datasets. *Dropout* is a popular regularization technique in deep learning in which random nodes of the neural network are ignored during forward passes. Weight decay is another regularization technique, one that adds a penalty term during training to encourage the model to learn "simpler" representations of the function they're modeling.

Step 3: Deploy and Maintain

A demo in a Google Colab notebook is fun, but the value to the business really comes by putting the model into production. Being "in production" can take many forms, from a batch Jenkins job that runs once a day to add the output of your model to the database to use for other purposes to a real-time streaming system where your deployed changes start impacting customers immediately. Here, we'll touch on some of the different aspects of your software where you're able to create CI/CD systems, and this will help you reduce human errors and streamline your processes.

- **Continuous integration/continuous delivery (CI/CD):** Implement CI/CD pipelines specifically tailored for ML model deployment. Automated deployment reduces errors and accelerates model deployment cycles. CI techniques include the following:

  - *Automated builds:* Automatically build the application when code changes are pushed to the version control system. This ensures that the code can be successfully compiled and that dependencies are resolved.

  - *Automated testing:* Execute automated tests (unit tests, integration tests, etc.) on the newly built code. Identify and address issues early in the development process, preventing integration problems later on.

  - *Version control integration:* Integrate CI with version control systems (e.g., Git). CI tools monitor repositories for changes and trigger the build and test process when new code is committed.

  - *Parallel test execution:* Execute tests in parallel to speed up the feedback loop. This helps reduce the time it takes to validate code changes, making the CI process more efficient.

  - *Artifact management:* Store and manage build artifacts, dependencies, and binaries in a repository. This ensures that the same artifacts are used consistently across different stages of the development pipeline.

- **CD techniques include the following:**

  - *Continuous deployment:* Extend continuous delivery to include automated deployment to production after passing all necessary tests. Continuous deployment aims to release new changes to production as quickly and reliably as possible.

- *Deployment automation:* Automate the deployment process to move code changes from development through to production environments. Deployment automation ensures consistency and reduces the risk of manual errors.

- *Environment configuration management:* Use infrastructure as code (IaC) to manage and version control the configuration of development, testing, and production environments. This helps maintain consistency and reproducibility across different environments.

- *Rollback mechanisms:* Implement automated rollback mechanisms in case a deployment introduces issues. This ensures that, in case of problems, the application can quickly and reliably revert to the previous version.

- *Feature toggles (feature flags):* Use feature toggles to enable or disable specific features in the application. This allows for the gradual rollout of new features and the ability to quickly disable them if issues arise.

- *Canary releases:* Deploy changes to a subset of users or servers before rolling them out to the entire user base. Canary releases help identify potential issues in a controlled environment and can be leveraged for hypothesis testing.

- **Automated database migrations:** Automate database schema updates and migrations as part of the deployment process. This ensures that database changes are applied consistently across environments. Database migration tools include the following:

  - *Jenkins:* Typically self-hosted, open-source, large community, and hundreds of plugins available for different tools and frameworks.

194

- *GitHub Actions:* Leverage "actions" to build a container, test, deploy a web service, or more, right from GitHub. Priced based on the amount of time your pipeline is running during the billing period, you get about 33 action hours per month for free.

- *GitLab CI/CD:* Cloud-based, provides distributed builds by default, limited set of integrations, requires external integrations through APIs.

- *AWS CodePipeline:* Included as part of the AWS free tier for one V1 type pipeline. Integrates with other AWS services.

- *Azure DevOps:* Cloud-based, end-to-end software development and delivery and offers agile project management, version control, and automated testing. Known for intuitive interface.

- *Travis CI:* Cloud-based, easy integration with GitHub workflows.

- *CircleCI:* Known for speed and efficiency, offering parallelism, caching, and containerization.

- **Monitoring and model maintenance:** Establish robust monitoring systems for model performance in production. Models degrade over time; continuous monitoring facilitates timely retraining and maintenance. Tools for model monitoring include the following:

  - *Aporia:* Offers models monitoring, but also offers guardrails for preventing inappropriate or undesired responses from LLMs and methods to avoid hallucinations.

  - *Comet:* Tool for tracking and visualizing your model at any scale, for any infrastructure. Also has functionality for logging and visualizing LLM prompts and chains.

- *TensorFlow Model Analysis:* Can be extended to support frameworks other than TensorFlow. Results can be visualized in a Jupyter notebook.

- *MLflow:* Open-source and probably the most popular tool for experiment tracking, but also offers model monitoring.

- *evidently.ai:* Open-source, ability to self-host your monitoring, evaluate, test, and monitor ML models for tabular, text, or embedding data.

These are just a few examples of the tools; there are more available. Most of these tools provide similar capabilities. Aporia also offers "guardrails" that provide the ability to control hallucinations, profanity, prompt injections, restricted topics, and which SQL tables are allowed to be used from a simple UI. This sets you up to be more proactive than reactive when managing the output of your LLMs.

Step 4: Collaborate and Communicate

Great collaboration and communication is necessary for a successful ML project. At the end of the day, analytics is a support function, and we're delivering models and products to meet the needs of the business. At the beginning of the project, you'll be collaborating to understand the scope and define the project, but at the end of the project, you'll be presenting your work to build trust in your results, get credit for your great work, and get buy-in on future iterations. Although this step is nontechnical, it's an art that can have a huge impact on your career.

- **Interdisciplinary collaboration:** Foster collaboration between data scientists, engineers, and domain experts. Diverse perspectives enhance model development and ensure alignment with business goals.

- **Clear communication of results:** Communicate model results and limitations effectively to nontechnical stakeholders, including the use of model interpretability and explainability techniques. Transparent communication fosters trust and informed decision-making.

The addition of MLOps principles and a focus on CI/CD equips data scientists for the realities of the direction that the field is moving. This book put a large focus on LLMs, a newly democratized capability that has recently been the focus of many organizations that want to leverage this technology. With the newfound popularity, there are a couple of emerging trends in LLMs that we wanted to mention.

Emerging Trends in LLMs

With great hype comes great responsibility. Although companies have been thinking about creating personalized customer experiences for more than a decade, preparing for the large volumes of customers interacting with LLMs provides a newer, more significant use case for optimizing latency at scale.

It has been an exciting time to be a data scientist. Figure 7.1 shows the demand of the term LLMs on Google Trends chart for the past three years.

One of the trends we're seeing is the rise of the "AI engineer" role. There has been a growing number of job titles in the data science world, and sometimes, it can be challenging to understand where one role might start and another begins. An AI engineer

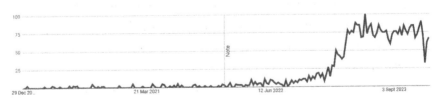

Figure 7.1 Google trends for LLM

Review of Best Practices

typically develops traditional ML models, or in the case of LLMs, they may be fine-tuning, building a RAG system, or building LLM-powered applications. AI engineers will have experience with the tools associated with LLMs, like LangChain and vector databases.

Speaking of vector databases, these are now having their day. LLMs often deal with high-dimensional data, such as word embeddings or feature vectors. Vector databases excel at performing similarity searches for semantically similar sentences or documents and allowing for quick and accurate retrieval of information. Vector databases are designed to scale horizontally, allowing for the efficient storage and retrieval of vectors across distributed systems and offering fast query performance. This makes them suitable for applications where low-latency responses are essential. Vector databases employ advanced indexing techniques, such as tree structures or hashing, to speed up search operations, making them great for handling the large-scale indexing requirements of LLMs. We covered vector databases in Chapter 3, "A Data-Centric View," but they represent a sector of the data ecosystem that is rapidly evolving and merits further study.

Beyond tooling, we also have to look forward at trends in the models themselves. For a long time now, models have been getting bigger as new models are released. There's even an entire school of thought following the so-called *scaling hypothesis*, which believes that the only thing between a modern LLM and AGI is scale. Following this logic, LLMs often have billions of parameters, as you can see by the most popular downloads on Hugging Face, as shown in Figure 7.2.

But over the last few years, we've seen a renewed interest in smaller, compressed models, which can be run more affordably. Sparsification tools or platforms such as Neural Magic emerged to help maintain a model's accuracy while reducing some of the complexity. Working with a smaller model will have obvious cost-saving benefits over time. Now the trend is not necessarily the largest model but to find a smaller model that offers the same benefits as some of the larger models to reduce cost.

Figure 7.2 Most popular LLM model downloads

Next Steps in Learning

In this book, we have given you an introduction to how you can start implementing different MLOps techniques, get started with LLMs, and create an app or API to deploy your work for end users. All of these topics go quite deep, and there are opportunities for further research. Some resources you might want to check out for deepening your understanding include the following:

- MLOps Community Slack

    This is a free community with more than 20,000 members. This is a great place to network, explore collaborations, get advice, and participate in discussions. The content in the community is most appropriate for intermediate to advanced MLOps practitioners.

Review of Best Practices

- Made with ML

  This is a tutorial series that includes MLOps at madewithml.com. "If you really need to focus on only one resource to build your end-to-end portfolio project, this is the resource you should be using. Period." This quote can be found at the bottom of Mikiko Bazeley's article at https://medium.com/kitchen-sink-data-science/mikis-hot-takes-on-mle-interviews-top-advice-resources-part-2-2-2004bb163b17.

- Deployment of Machine Learning Models

  This is a Udemy course created by Soledad Galli, PhD, and Christopher Samiullah. Udemy is an online learning platform. This course covers deployment into a production environment, using Docker to control software and model versions, and adding CI/CD, etc.

- ML System Design Case Studies

  Evidently AI (https://evidentlyai.com/ml-system-design) has put together 300 case studies when companies have shared about their ML systems created in-house, the ML model design, evaluation criteria, and implementation. Thirty-six of the cases involve NLP.

Thank you for coming on this journey with us. We hope you've gained a new perspective on tracking your experiments, learned skills for prompting and leveraging LLMs, and better understand what is required to build your API. We wrote this book because we love data science and feel so fortunate to be a part of the evolution and transformation of the field over time. We wish you success in your career and hope you find it as fulfilling as we do.

Additional LLM Example

This appendix provides an additional example and is also available on the book's GitHub. This example will use data that you'd like to leverage along with the large language model (LLM). For the purposes of this example, we'll be using two blog articles, and we'll create an email based specifically on the information provided. The real-world example would be for a company that has to create a lot of content for their customers. They want the information in those emails to reflect the content that they're looking to share. But trying to put this all into the prompt window would become impossible if you wanted to create content around a large number of topics; this data needs to be stored in a database.

You could also add drop-downs so that the audience, channel, etc., matches the type of customer you want to reach.

Just like with everything else, we'll need to `pip install` our packages first.

```
!pip install langchain==0.1.5 \
  openai==1.11.1 \
  pymilvus==2.3.6 \
  gradio==4.16.0 \
  langchain_openai==0.0.5 \
  pyarrow==14.0.0
```

You'll want to restart the runtime now. Next you'll read the CSV, and you'll want to place the data in files at the same level as the `sample data` folder. Then you'll use Pandas to read the CSV.

```
import pandas as pd
# Read CSV file into a DataFrame
df = pd.read_csv('demo_data.csv')
```

The following block of code is similar to the original YouTube transcription example. You need to import some libraries, create variables for your API keys, and create the schema for the articles that you're uploading. In this case, the fields are for the ID, author, text, and associated vector. You'll create the index for the collection and then iterate through the rows to append information and create the vector embeddings.

Once you've run this cell, you'll need to navigate to `zilliz.com` to load the data into your database so that you can later retrieve it.

```
from pymilvus import (
    Collection,
    CollectionSchema,
    connections,
    DataType,
    FieldSchema,
    utility,
    MilvusClient
)
from openai import OpenAI

COLLECTION_NAME = 'content'   # Collection name
EMBEDDING_DIMENSION = 1536   # Embedding vector size,
specified by OpenAI
```

```
ZILLIZ_CLLUSTER_URI = 'YOUR_ZILLIZ_URI'  # Endpoint
URI obtained from Zilliz Cloud
ZILLIZ_API_KEY = 'YOUR_ZILLIZ_API_KEY'
OPENAI_API_KEY = 'YOUR_OPENAI_API_KEY'
connections.connect(uri=ZILLIZ_CLLUSTER_URI, token=
ZILLIZ_API_KEY, secure=True)


## If the data already exists, drop it so we don't end
## up pushing up duplicates
if utility.has_collection(COLLECTION_NAME):
    utility.drop_collection(COLLECTION_NAME)
# Create collection which includes the id, title,
## and embedding.
fields = [
  FieldSchema(name='id', dtype=DataType.VARCHAR,
is_primary=True, auto_id=True, max_length=36),
  FieldSchema(name='author', dtype=DataType.VARCHAR,
max_length=200),
  FieldSchema(name='text', dtype=DataType.VARCHAR,
max_length=2000),
  FieldSchema(name='vector', dtype=DataType.FLOAT_
VECTOR, dim=EMBEDDING_DIMENSION)
]
schema = CollectionSchema(fields=fields)
collection = Collection(name=COLLECTION_NAME,
schema=schema)
# Create an index for the collection.
index_params = {
    'index_type': 'AUTOINDEX',
    'metric_type': 'IP',
    'params': {}
}
```

Appendix: Additional LLM Example

```
collection.create_index(field_name="vector",
index_params=index_params)
milvusClient = MilvusClient(
    uri=ZILLIZ_CLLUSTER_URI,
    token=ZILLIZ_API_KEY)
openAIClient = OpenAI(api_key=OPENAI_API_KEY)
```

Next, we'll initialize a list to store data that will be inserted into the collection. Then we're iterating through rows of the dataframe and appends information as a dictionary. Giving us a list of dictionaries.

```
rows = []
for row in df.to_records():
  rows.append({
      'author': row[1],
      'text': row[2],
      'vector': openAIClient.embeddings.create(
          input=row[2],
          model='text-embedding-ada-002').data[0]
.embedding
  })
## inserts the data in "rows" into the collection
milvusClient.insert(COLLECTION_NAME, rows)
```

In the next block, you're setting up a pipeline for generating responses to questions using a combination of information retrieval from a Milvus collection and response generation from an OpenAI model. Here, you'll import various modules and classes for interacting with FAISS, OpenAI, and Milvus. Then you'll establish connections to external services like the Zilliz cluster using your URI and API key. The ZillizRetriever class executes a search query on the collection based on the provided query and returns relevant documents. The get_response function includes retrieving the relevant documents based on the retriever, formatting the prompt template, generating a response from the OpenAI model, and parsing the output. Finally, it returns the response generated by the model. You can enter any language.

```
from operator import itemgetter
import os
from langchain_community.vectorstores import FAISS
from langchain_core.output_parsers import
StrOutputParser
from langchain_core.prompts import ChatPromptTemplate
from langchain_core.runnables import RunnableLambda,
RunnablePassthrough
from langchain_openai import ChatOpenAI,
OpenAIEmbeddings
from langchain_community.vectorstores import Milvus
from langchain.globals import set_debug, set_verbose
from langchain_core.retrievers import BaseRetriever
from langchain_core.documents import Document
from langchain_core.callbacks import
CallbackManagerForRetrieverRun
from openai import OpenAI
from typing import List
from pymilvus import (
    connections,
    MilvusClient
)
set_verbose(True)
os.environ['OPENAI_API_KEY'] = OPENAI_API_KEY
connections.connect(uri=ZILLIZ_CLLUSTER_URI,
token=ZILLIZ_API_KEY, secure=True)
milvusClient = MilvusClient(
    uri=ZILLIZ_CLLUSTER_URI,
    token=ZILLIZ_API_KEY)
```

```python
class ZillizRetriever(BaseRetriever):
    def _get_relevant_documents(
        self, query: str, *, run_manager:
CallbackManagerForRetrieverRun
    ) -> List[Document]:
        results = milvusClient.search(
            collection_name=COLLECTION_NAME,
            data = [openAIClient.embeddings.create
(input=query,

model='text-embedding-ada-002').data[0].embedding],
            limit=3,
            output_fields=["author", "text"])
        docs = []
        for result in results[0]:
            doc = Document(page_content=result
['entity']['text'])
            docs.append(doc)
        return docs


def get_response(question, language):
  retriever = ZillizRetriever()

  template = """Answer the question based only on the
following context and formatted as an email:
  {context}
  Question: {question}
  Answer in the following language: {language}
  """
  prompt = ChatPromptTemplate.from_template(template)
  model = ChatOpenAI()
  chain = (
      {
```

```
        "context": itemgetter("question") |
retriever,
        "question": itemgetter("question"),
        "language": itemgetter("language"),
    }
      | prompt
      | model
      | StrOutputParser()
  )
  return chain.invoke({'question': question,
'language': language})

#chain.invoke({'question': "What is the focus for this
year?", 'language': 'english'})
```

You're now ready to create the app. Import gradio and then use the Interface function to create the demo app.

```
import gradio as gr
iface = gr.Interface(
    fn=get_response,
    inputs=["text", "text"],
    outputs="text",
    live=True,
    title="Content App",
    description="Ask a question for killer content",
)
iface.launch()
```

Ideally, having this additional example will help you see how you could build out any number of different use cases. If you'd like to add a submit button or build this out further, refer to Chapter 5, "Putting Together an Application."

Index

Index

data versioning
about, 50–53
getting started with, 53–57
databases
automated migrations for, 194–195
vector, 13, 31, 34–49, 198
data-centric view
about, 25
building datasets, 30–57
data ethics, 28–30
data-driven approach, 28
emergence of foundation
models, 25–27
engineering, 57–60
role of off-the-shelf
components, 27–28
data-driven approach, 28
datasets
building, 30–57
data management, 50–53
data versioning, 50–53
working with vector
databases, 34–49
Davinci, 44
deep learning models, 35–36
defining
Agent class, 99–102
feedback routes, 177–180
prediction routes, 177–180
deploy and maintain step, 192–196
deploying
automation of, as a continuous
deployment (CD)
technique, 194
large language models
(LLMs), 154–159
models as APIs, 144–149
simple random forest
models, 161–166
as a step in CRISP-DM, 5
Deployment of Machine Learning
Models Udemy course, 200

developer focus, as a benefit of
deploying models as APIs, 124
developer-friendliness, as a benefit
of deploying models as
APIs, 124–125
DevOps, 156
Docker, 151–153, 200
Docker Compose, 153
DockerHub, 151–153
dockerizing services, 151–153
domain-specific tasks, fine-tuning
for, 112–113
drift, 174
dropout, 192

E
embedding text, 35–36
embeddings storage, 14
emerging trends in LLMs step, 197–199
end-to-end approach
about, 11–13
principles of a production machine
learning system, 16–24
YouTube search agent, 13–16
.env file, 149, 153
environment configuration
management, as a
continuous deployment (CD)
technique, 194
ethical considerations/governance, 6
Euclidean distance, 37
evaluation, as a step in CRISP-DM, 5
evidently.ai
about, 196, 200
model monitoring with, 175–176
experiment
about, 9, 69
management, optimizing LLM
inference with, 102–111
management of, with large language
models (LLMs), 68–74

213

215

"Universal Language Model Fine-
Tuning for Text Classification"
(Howard and Ruder), 63–64
University of Tokyo, 87
Unsupervised Multitask Learners, 63–64
usability, as a benefit of deploying
models as APIs, 125
user interface, 15
user needs, as a benefit of deploying
models as APIs, 125
utility script, 164
Uvicorn, implementing, 148–149

web framework, 146
websites
Deployment of Machine
Learning Models Udemy
course, 200
Evidently AI, 200
Made with ML tutorial, 200
QLOrA GitHub repository, 114
Zilliz, 39
weight decay, 192
Wilkinson, Leland (author)
Grammar of Graphics,
128–129
Wolpert, David (mathematician), 62

V

vector databases
about, 13, 31, 198
working with, 34–49
version control
about, 9
integration of, as a continuous
integration (CI) technique, 193
visualization, breakdown of, 129
visualization library, 12
vLLM, 154–155, 176

X

x-axis, 128

Y

YAML, 157–158
y-axis, 128
YouTube retrieval, 14
YouTube search agent
components, 13–16
YouTubeReceiver, 90–94

W

Walton, Nick (researcher), 21–22
warmup steps, 192
Weapons of Math Destruction
(O'Neil), 30

Z

"zero-shot-CoT," 87
Zilliz, 22, 24, 36, 39–49, 204